BOSTON'S FADING INK

BOSTON'S FADING INK

A Journalist's Path Through the Final Good Years of HUB NEWSPAPERS

DYKE HENDRICKSON

AMERICA
THROUGH
TIME

America Through Time®
An imprint of Sutton Publishing inc
www.through-time.com

First published 2025

ISBN 978-1-63499-513-9

Typeset in 10.5pt on 13pt Sabon
Printed and bound in England

Contents

1

Mixing with Newsmakers

It was 1987, and the press party was at the Rainbow Room, a luxury New York retreat high above Radio City Music Hall. Gathered were executives and TV stars from the ABC network. The media had been invited to talk with the personalities, so scribes and TV reporters would have fodder to put into news stories and TV shorts.

I saw Roone Arledge, network president, and Barbara Walters, a Boston-bred newscaster, standing near the restaurant's immense windows that looked over Manhattan. You could also behold distant Hoboken, N.J.

I quickly walked up to the pair, hoping to get a few words in before the horde noticed them. "Roone," I said jauntily, "that is a fine tie you are wearing."

Arledge, on the short side and a bit rotund, was ready for questions. But about his tie? He looked at Walters and then back at me, as if to say, "This is a dark blue tie with a few white dots ..."

And then he noticed that I was wearing the exact same tie. He smiled, shook my hand, and said, "Yes, we both have great taste in neck wear."

Barbara Walters looked at my press badge, which identified me as the TV editor of the *Boston Herald*. She said, "How is Rupert Murdoch treating you? I'm from Boston, as you might know, and I hope he doesn't ruin one of the only remaining papers in town."

I smiled. "Rupert wants the best for Boston. And he wants a lot of coverage of television. That is why I am here."

She smiled and she extended her hand.

This was good. We chatted a few minutes longer about what ABC had coming up that season. And then we were joined by TV reporters from Chicago, Atlanta or wherever.

I listened for a while and then walked off to look at gaze through the sixty-fifth-floor windows at New Jersey, my inglorious home state. I had never expected to be clinking glasses with two of the most significant figures in American television of the '80s. But I liked it. I also liked the fact that the headquarters of the national TV press tour that I was attending was the Waldorf-Astoria Hotel. I never had expected to be staying for two weeks at the Waldorf. On the company dime.

But that's what a press pass can do.

This retrospective represents a bittersweet recollection of a newspaper career that spanned more than forty years. My career never ascended to the heights of stars like *The Washington Post*'s Bob Woodward or *The Boston Globe*'s Bud Collins, but it was highly interesting. I covered sports, news, music, ethnicity, and politics in my early years and high tech, medical research, and the development of the internet in my later career. I have written seven books.

I had not anticipated such an interesting, entertaining career. I was a history major at little-known Franklin and Marshall College in Pennsylvania. Unlike many media luminaries, there was no internship or summer job at a newspaper for me.

During college, I was too diffident to lead anything more than a trip to downtown Lancaster for a case of beer. If there was a game plan senior year in 1967, it was to avoid going to Vietnam.

But as any septuagenarian will tell you, a lot of things happen in a lifetime. Jobs were found. Jobs were lost. Families were raised. Much good fortune was encountered.

During the COVID-19, many Americans were locked down. Home-bound baby boomers started thinking about what had happened in their lives. How did the career go? Had I enjoyed my five decades of adulthood? How is the family?

I was in big-time media, but I was not an investigative reporter. The term "investigative reporter" is used frequently in the lexicon of journalism, but these individuals are rare. It takes special circumstances to become one. At the least, it requires committed editors who support stories that might lead to lawsuits. And it requires the reporter to have a thick skin. Individuals or organizations that are burned by journalists push back with vigor.

Features, profiles, and historical narrative flowed from my typewriter, later a laptop. Newspapers that offered full-time employment included the *Portland Press Herald*, the *New Orleans Times-Picayune*, the *Boston Herald*, and the *Boston Business Journal*. My last paper was the hometown *The Daily News* of Newburyport.

As a reporter, I covered presidents Jimmy Carter and George W. Bush, interviewed tennis stars Billie Jean King and Jimmy Connors, and I was flattered when World Wide Web creator Tim Berners-Lee returned my calls. As a traveling scribe, I covered the Super Bowl in Miami, Wimbledon in London, the Grammys in New York and the television industry in Hollywood. Now I am writing environmental books about rivers and barrier islands.

From the age of twelve, I wanted to be a journalist.

As a young man, I was like Walter Mitty. I dreamed big dreams, musing about being a foreign correspondent or a popular TV anchor. But I slowly learned that would not happen. So, I went into newspapers and observed—often on scene—many talented celebrities of the day.

As part of the connected world of journalism, I also served as a communications manager for Massachusetts General Hospital and as a public relations director for a wacky internet start-up called Wired Empire. I was an upwardly mobile liberal arts major in a world that was heading toward technology. I was able to land a lot of jobs, in a wide variety of fields. And I lost quite a few.

The second half of my career took place as the newspaper business was collapsing.

A lot of people want to be writers. Many never get published. Yet in the newspaper business, everything I wrote for four decades was published. I took risks to get jobs, and sometimes I paid for it. We moved often, which my children remember with some chagrin. But it was very interesting and brought more adventures than I could have imagined.

To paraphrase the oft-overlooked American writer Anita Loos, "Fate kept coming at me." Much of my career—twenty years—was working for Boston newspapers. I was there at a peak—the mid-'80s—and present when they began declining, in about 2002. I was with the *Boston Herald*, *Mass High Tech*, and the *Woburn Advocate*. (Note: *Mass High Tech* was a sister newspaper to the *Boston Business Journal*. *Mass High Tech* folded years ago. I will use the term *Boston Business Journal* because readers won't recognize *MHT*).

My last full-time job was with *The Daily News* of Newburyport, Mass., where my wife, Vicki, and I live today. I wrote there from 2012 to 2017. Now I am writing books with maritime themes and the occasional feature story for this newspaper.

In 2025, the financial viability of print journalism continues to fall. But even as newspapers fade, though, the opportunities in electronic media are proliferating.

The number of print publications drops each year. Four of the publications for which I wrote have folded. Three major newspapers that employed me (*Press Herald*, *Boston Herald*, *The Times-Picayune*) are struggling. Each has been forced to move out of their buildings. Real estate is worth much more than the newspaper company. Many local publications can barely meet their payrolls.

But let's reminisce, not lament.

Good years stretched from 1970 to 2002. This final surge for newspapers starts with the Watergate reporting and goes the year *The Boston Globe* published its award-winning series about sexual abuse in the Catholic Church.

At that time, I was most interested in sports. The *Globe* provided great newspaper coverage of its popular pro teams. The *Globe* had fine sportswriters, including Ray Fitzgerald, Larry Whiteside, Leigh Montville, Leslie Visser, Bob Ryan, Will McDonough, and Dan Shaughnessy.

Sports aside, its series on the church in about 2002 was likely the best investigative work in the past century.

Though the *New York Times* has earned more Pulitzer Prizes than the *Globe*, it must be remembered that these awards come out of Columbia University. *Times* executives and editors teach at Columbia and are the most influential in naming winners. The *Globe*'s damning series about the church was lionized in the movie *Spotlight*. That film won the Academy Award for Best Motion Picture in 2015, and it is a brilliant portrayal of the creation of that series.

The *Boston Herald* was also a player in the '80s and '90s. It served as the springboard for publisher Rupert Murdoch to enter the American market. He bought the *Herald* in 1982. He also owned the *New York Post* and *New York* magazine. From here he became a dominant player on the national scene by developing the conservative Fox television network.

The *Herald*'s Howie Carr was, and is, the best reporter of his era, and that includes all the *Globe*'s well-paid stars. He has written hundreds of stories about malfeasance in the state capital. In his body of work, he produced shocking tales about the Bulger brothers, one a murderer and the other a political rogue.

Certainly, Carr was the bravest scribe to ever ply the trade in modern Boston. He wrote fearlessly about hitmen and mobsters and has commented he has been lucky to live through it. Carr has developed a national following with his conservative radio program. Despite writing provocative stories that made powerful men furious, he was a very accurate reporter.

Boston's Fading Ink notes that the hard-copy product is diminishing. But other opportunities are available.

Young people should know that journalism is still a vibrant and exciting field. Online communications companies have hired thousands. Corporations, colleges, and government officials require the skills of journalists. Well-constructed podcasts thrive. It's just that a part of the print era is concluding. Newspapers are yesterday's news.

2

Names Make News

Journalists like superlatives, the "best" this and the "most memorable" that.

Here are some reflections on the most exciting events and the most intriguing people I met. None of this would have happened without a press pass.

Notable events from which I filed stories: National Mayors Conference, San Francisco, 1971; Mexico City News desk, 1971; New England Patriots coverage in seasons, 1972–1976; U.S. Senate race, Margaret Chase Smith *v.* Bill Hathaway, 1972; Kentucky Derby, 1973; Wimbledon, 1974; Super Bowl, 1976; presidential race, Jimmy Carter, 1976; Senate race, Edmund Muskie, 1976; tennis championships, Longwood, Forest Hills, Flushing Meadows, 1978–1998; Grammys, 1979; horrific plane crash in New Orleans, 1983; World's Fair, 1984; TV industry in Hollywood, 1984–90; development of World Wide Web, Boston, 1996–2006; national high-tech conferences in New York, Chicago, San Francisco, 1998; presidential race, Al Gore and George Bush, 2000; medical breakthroughs in Cambridge, 2000–2006; national medical conferences, Mass General Hospital, 2007; presidential race, Mitt Romney, 2008; hosting novelist Tess Gerritsen, documentary maker Rachel Slade and Sen. George Mitchell at Newburyport Literary Festival, 2005–2022.

The following are some of the most interesting public figures encountered.

Arthur Ashe: Arthur was a tennis titan, but he was very reserved in person. I met him in the '70s in Newport, R.I., during the Hall of Fame tournament and again in North Conway, N.H., in that era for the Volvo International event. North Conway is in the White Mountains. Asked by a local reporter to extrapolate on the beauty of the area, Arthur lamely responded, "If you've seen one great mountain, you've seen them all." He was not a quote-meister who loudly lauded each tournament. In real life, of course, Arthur was courageous. During the fight for racial equality in South Africa and other places, he was jailed on numerous occasions. He never gave up. Versatile and fluent, he wrote several well-regarded volumes on the history of black athletes. More on Arthur later.

Ken Burns: Ken, the historian and TV producer, is one of the best communicators in the business. When he appeared at PBS events that I covered as TV editor of the *Boston Herald*, he was prepared, provocative and willing to answer all questions. He is revered for his work on the "Civil War," but his most informative work was about the Roosevelts. Also, his ten-part series on Vietnam was admirably comprehensive. It was special because many of the interviews were with former members of the Viet Cong and the North Vietnam Army.

George W. Bush: Bush was a likable guy I covered in 2000 because he spent much time in nearby New Hampshire in preparation for the presidential primaries. But he was the worst president ever. And that includes the oft-mentioned holder of that title, James Buchanan, 1856–1860. In 2020, PBS produced a special on the "elective wars" in Iraq and Afghanistan that were engineered by this President Bush. PBS reported that American armed forces killed 130,000 Iraqis and maimed three times that number. Reporters interviewed Iraqis who had lost arms, legs, eyes and many other parts because this inexperienced GOP president was "acting from my gut." I also covered Al Gore, his opponent, in 2000. Gore was funny and informative when he appeared at MIT in 1999. Gore was unfairly diminished in the media for "being boring."

Bill Cosby: He was an entertaining interview, always throwing out one-liners as if he were doing stand-up. His *The Cosby Show* was just hitting the heights in the late '80s, when I was covering the television industry in Hollywood. He had finally made it; he was among the top names in Hollywood. As Dr. Cliff Huxtable, he was determined to be part of an accurate, entertaining series. His producers often brought along doctors and child psychiatrists to stress the veracity of his show's scripts. He did a lot right. But he assaulted women. In 2021, he was released from prison on an appeal.

The belligerent Bob Carmichael: Bob was a minor Australian tennis player who played a tournament in Portland, Maine, in the '70s. I was a sportswriter with the *Portland Press Herald*. He got annoyed after reading a story I wrote. He approached me and said, "Let's go outside and we'll sort this out with fists." I stuck to my chair in the press area like a mannequin sitting in Super Glue. In truth, I was a little too glib in my coverage. In my late twenties, I was trying to become the Bud Collins of northern New England.

Jimmy Carter: Carter came out of nowhere in the '70s to win the Democratic nomination for president. He was not a compelling speaker. He was not amusing. Carter was not even interesting. But he was a hard worker and united the Democrats in 1976. I interviewed him in Biddeford, Maine, during the primary. After he won the nomination, I spoke with him at the Portland airport. He knew his talking points, but in the age of television, he must have been the least dynamic president of the late twentieth century. He beat Gerald Ford, who made history (and many enemies) by pardoning the rogue Richard Nixon.

Bud Collins: Collins, *The Boston Globe*'s sportswriter and prominent TV commentator, was probably the nicest guy in sports journalism. He welcomed everyone. Just minutes before a big 100th anniversary Davis Cup match in

Boston between the U.S. and Australia, he risked tardiness by giving an interview to a high school journalist outside of the Longwood club in Boston. Bud was the spark plug in the press room at every tournament he covered. He organized tennis tournaments for reporters; he led conga lines at parties given for players and/or members of the media. He remembered names and sent cards on birthdays. He was beloved by players and fans alike. He died in 2016.

Jimmy Connors: Conners was one of the most difficult public sports figures of his day. He disliked the media. When I asked him for an interview at a tournament in Maui in 1978, his first response was, "Why should I talk to you?" He was not smiling. This was not a promising start to an interview. But after I explained the story that I wanted to write, we spoke for about a half-hour. It was a piece for the magazine run by the Association of Tennis Professionals (ATP). Connors was not a member of the ATP. He was feuding with its top leaders such as Arthur Ashe and Stan Smith. My story reflected the reasons Connors did not join the ATP. In that way, the story served Connors.

Robert Duvall: Duvall the actor was highly entertaining when he spoke about his many roles, from *The Godfather* to *Lonesome Dove*. He spoke to reporters during the media party for *Lonesome Dove* in 1988. He is a great dancer! A one-on-one interview with Duvall is chronicled in a later part of this tome.

Bill Gates: A great news source when he wanted to be. I covered technology and medicine for more than a decade (1996–2006) for what was *Mass High Tech*. This weekly newspaper was closed and then folded into the current *Boston Business Journal*. For the purpose of clarity, I say that I worked for the *Business Journal*. Gates was effective with the media. He could be funny (for a tech guy). Here's a memory from when he received an honorary degree from Harvard, from which he had dropped out as an undergraduate. He quipped, "Now that I am changing fields [he was entering the world of philanthropy], I guess it's good that I finally have a college degree."

Audrey Hepburn: A great actress and an elegant public figure. She was much loved for her work with UNICEF in the final years of her life. She will be described in another part of this book. She was one of the most revered actors ever in Hollywood.

Sen. Ted Kennedy: Ted Kennedy never won the presidency. But he left his mark as having been a very productive senator. He was always entertaining. In the Sanford, Maine, high school gym in about 1976, he was campaigning for Sen. Edmund Muskie. The gymnasium was packed. People were screaming. After energetically walking down the center aisle of the small gymnasium, he strode to the podium, and asked, in French, "Is Sanford going to beat Biddeford (in football) on Saturday?" (Sanford and Biddeford were mill communities with many French-Canadian immigrants). The resulting roar, in the affirmative, was "Oui! Oui!"

Billie Jean King: She has spent an enormous amount of time with the media. She provided thoughtful answers to difficult questions. The great pathfinder in women's tennis once remarked, "During a lot of my playing years, I was giving interviews on women's rights, not practicing. I bet I could have been better if I had practiced more." I had lunch with her in about 1989 at the *Boston Herald*. She was seeking funding from newspaper owner Rupert Murdoch for her fledgling World Team Tennis. I was brought into the lunch by publisher Pat Purcell, who didn't know anything about tennis. I said to Billie Jean, "I loved your victory over Evonne Goolagong in 1974. You were down 3-0 in the third but pulled it out." She smiled broadly. "That is one of my favorite matches. I'll never forget it. You really know your tennis." I remembered that match at Forest Hills, because my mother, Eloise Hendrickson, was dying of cancer at our home in Demarest, N.J., at that time. My father and I had taken a break from our around-the-clock care and had left my mother with nurses. My father, Clint Hendrickson, and I had gone to the matches for the afternoon.

John McEnroe: He played in Portland during the spring of '78. He was unknown. That summer he would reach the semi-finals of Wimbledon. He became a national name after that. In Portland, he had very little to say because he had done very little at that time. Tournament director Gene Scott said McEnroe was going to be great. He was right. McEnroe was eighteen when he played in the Down East Tennis Classic. His left-handed serve was the most remarkable thing about his game. On grass, his slice to the ad court was unreachable for most opponents. He was the greatest volleyer of his day, and they used small rackets in the '70s. He won seventy-seven singles tournaments and seventy-eight doubles tournaments, mostly with partner Peter Fleming, a 6-foot 5-inch, one-time UCLA standout.

Bob Metcalfe: Metcalfe was a luminary who was a columnist for several national tech magazines, was friendly and informative. His key vocations were investor and facilitator. He had degrees from both MIT and Harvard, and he was a keynoter for many high-tech programs in the Boston area from 1995 to 2000. Metcalfe held frequent salons at his beautiful townhouse on Beacon Street, Boston. He welcomed the media. But he only served white wine. Never red. He insisted that media members were careless, and that spilled (red) wine would ruin his rugs and furniture. He and his wife had a farm in coastal Lincolnville, Maine.

Gov. Janet Mills: Mills was the first female governor of Maine as well as the first woman attorney general of that state. Janet married once, to a widower with five daughters. She had been a very unorthodox political figure who would be worthy of a biography.

Sen. George Mitchell: Sen. Mitchell of Maine was one of the most noble public figures of his day. He was thoughtful. He was clever. He was an unobtrusive but consistent achiever. Because we lived in Waterville, Maine, in the early '90s, I would interview him for *The Morning Sentinel* there when he was a Senate majority leader. In 1996, he left the Senate. He served as a mediator for the U.S. government and helped bring peace to Northern Ireland. Our daughter, Leslie, served as a Senate page under Mitchell in the '90s. Every year I send him a birthday card, and he reciprocates. We were both born on August 20. (So was Connie Chung.)

Sen. Edmund Muskie: Muskie ran for reelection in 1976. When I was with the *Portland Press Herald*, I was assigned to cover him for a day. It was one of those, "Get in the car, and get some quotes" type of assignments. Muskie was not very talkative with a cub reporter. The journey included a visit to a small factory in South Paris, Maine, that should probably have been shut down for housing flammable compounds. Workers painted sleds. There was so much paint and thinner compound in the air that visitors gagged when they entered the poorly ventilated mill. When we left, everyone, including Muskie, started laughing uncontrollably. We were probably high on fumes.

Like Ted Kennedy, Muskie was a great senator, if never president. He led the initiatives for the Clean Air Act in 1971 and the Clean Water Act of 1972. Muskie wasn't successful as either a vice-presidential candidate or a presidential hopeful, but in terms of the environment, he was a great contributor to the national good.

Martina Navratilova: The great tennis champion—and now commentator—played team tennis for the Boston Lobsters in the '70s. In about 1975, I made a request to see her after a Lobsters' match at Boston University. The PR lady must have miscommunicated my request. The message that Martina received was, "There's a dyke out there waiting in the press room." Martina was young and had not yet come out. When she arrived in the press room, she had an air of expectation that she was going to see a young woman. She encountered only me. She said diffidently, "I heard there was someone waiting for me." "Yes, that would be me." Her eyes widened; she was nonplussed. "Was there a woman here?" "No." "What is your name?" "Dyke Hendrickson." "Dyke? Is that your name?" she asked in a high, strangled voice. "Yes, Dyke Hendrickson, from Portland, Maine." She paused, and finally said, "I can't believe any parent would name their child Dyke." She sighed and sat down in a nearby chair. The interview, which started so awkwardly, did not go well. Dyke is my name. It is not a nickname. I have only met one other Dyke. That was at the bar of a restaurant in Camden, Maine, years ago. The fellow was in construction. When he introduced himself, I blurted out, "I can't believe that is your name. Do you have a card?" He pulled one out, and there it was. Not a nickname. A name. The name Dyke is Dutch, as are the Hendricksons. Evidently my parents knew a tennis player in California named Dyke. After my (older) sister was named Dale, Clint and Eloise went with Dyke. Dale and Dyke.

Oprah and Ted Turner: They were energetic spellbinders at press conferences. Every project that Oprah undertook seemed to turn to gold. The gregarious Turner recognized reporters by name, which all insecure scribes appreciate. Oprah and Ted made periodic visits to the press tour in L.A. during the '80s. Of course, they are pioneers of their era.

Robert Parker: The popular Boston-area writer created *Spenser: For Hire*, starring the late Robert Urich. It was a TV series that lasted about five seasons. Parker lived in Cambridge. He was trotted out on numerous occasions for the Boston media. He and his wife had occasional problems. The story went that they lived in the same large house but had separate entrances. If one did not want to see the other, they would keep their door locked. Talking about Urich, he was a very friendly guy. He was cooperative with the media before dying at fifty-six. Burt Reynolds, who had gone to Florida State University with Urich, said Urich was one of the few people he knew that never said a bad word about anyone.

Dolly Parton: A terrific communicator. With about five dozen other scribes, I met her at the California Yacht Club in 1989. She visited every table and shook every hand. She had something different to say to everyone. What a hard-working, capable entertainer. Another non-stop promoter was Bob Hope, whose L.A. home the scribes visited in the late '80s.

Rick Pitino: A basketball coach who coached at both the professional and college level, Pitino was impossible. He was the most uncooperative celebrity I ever interviewed. I was invited to hear him at an investors' conference in Boston in about 1999. Pitino, who coached the Celtics, was at a small gathering among execs to address the subject of motivation. I had been invited by a PR firm to talk with him. He knew that. But he acted like such an asshole. "Why would you ask that question?" he would say without warmth. "Why would you need to know that?" Perhaps his anti-social approach to the media was part of the reason he got fired in Boston, and later, at Louisville.

Mitt Romney: The senator was energetic and informed. He would have an answer for every question. In about 2003, he was governor of Massachusetts and touting its prowess in high tech. He developed a very progressive health-insurance program for Massachusetts. But he had to almost disavow it when GOP leaders turned more conservative.

Renee Richards: Tennis player Renee Richards spent much of her tennis career discussing her personal life. She was the first public transexual in sports and had a lot of explaining to do. Renee accommodated the media. In later years, interviews with her son suggested he had grown up angry because she had spent too much time focused on her own life. He said he would have appreciated spending more time with her. More will be said about her later in this tale.

Pete Rozelle: NFL commissioner Pete Rozelle could answer any question out there. At the Super Bowl in Miami in 1976, the former marketing manager was a spellbinder when dealing with the media before the Dallas-Pittsburgh game. He was an effective figurehead for football. It is said that the NFL took a large leap forward because of his leadership.

Alex Trebek: TV host Alex Trebek once called me at the *Boston Herald* to complain that I had released "private" information about upcoming shows for *Jeopardy*. He was furious. Yet he had given me the info several days earlier during a phone interview. The session was not off the record. When one watches the old shows, he seems like a nice guy. But he evidently could muster great rage over nothing.

John Walsh: A mourning parent and TV figure. He starred on the TV series *America's Most Wanted* after his young son, Adam, was abducted and murdered. The gravitas of his personal situation made him a great host for a much-watched program. He was a natural on TV.

Serena Williams: She can be fiery on the court, but she is soft-spoken and cooperative with the media. My years of interviewing her were 2003–2006. Venus Williams was an effective voice for women's tennis and also cooperative with journalists.

3

Before Newspapers, a VISTA Volunteer

In 1967, healthy young men faced a challenge. Males between eighteen and twenty-six were being drafted into the army. The Vietnam War was accelerating.

The war itself was a costly mistake for America. It was very expensive in blood, treasure, and world leadership. But that was not apparent in 1967, my graduation year.

The news clips will show that, nationally, there was much protesting in the streets during the late '60s, but it was not everywhere. There was not one protest in Lancaster, Pennsylvania, during my time there. I was captain of the tennis team, a reveler at the Chi Phi fraternity house, and an average history student. The war was not a daily part of most collegiate lives.

But when students considered their futures, the Vietnam War cast a dark shadow on every U.S. campus. Several grads from my alma mater, Northern Valley Regional High School in Demarest, N.J., were killed. A couple guys returned to our college homecoming in wheelchairs after surviving serious wounds. I did not want to go into the army.

The most relevant comment from an anti-war protester was, "How can you ask a soldier to be the last guy to die for a mistake?" The speaker was decorated veteran and one-time U.S. Sen. John Kerry. Post-college life included avoiding the draft.

Today, it is not fashionable to say you wanted to avoid the draft. That's because those who did evade the military machine do not talk about it. But millions of men did avoid military service, which was not new. During the Civil War, for instance, a prospective soldier could pay another to take his place. President Theodore Roosevelt's father did, which made Teddy the Warmonger a little embarrassed in later years.

Federal officials in the 1960s did not permit payments to substitutes, but they did create deferments for non-military projects such as the Peace Corps and VISTA (Volunteers in Service to America). There were also deferments for those working in the inner city for the greater social good.

Regarding jobs for "the greater social good," I applied for a government position as a social worker in Manhattan. The job description stated that the successful candidate would go into Harlem and the Bronx to talk with drug abusers and/or traffickers who were thought to be spreading sexually transmitted diseases.

Dressed in a blue summer suit, college rep tie, and glossy wingtips, I tried to explain to my interviewer that I was the right candidate. He knew this was a farce, but he played it straight. "Do you think you will want to leave comfortable Bergen County every evening to walk the streets here, and ask parolees and drug addicts about their sex habits? You believe that they will confide in you?"

The answer: no job.

After graduation, applications went to the Peace Corps, VISTA, and the Shell Oil Co. training program. Why Shell? My parents were life-long Republicans, and I needed some conversational cover.

While waiting for the draft board to find me, I got a job as bar waiter at the Monmouth Hotel in Spring Lake, N.J. The previous summer, I had been a bartender and room-service waiter at the Samoset Hotel in Rockland, Maine. Money could be saved in Maine because management provided room and board.

Long before promoters of Maine came up with the phase, this was "Life as it Should Be."

The owners of the hotel liked me because I was a good doubles partner. There were lots of cute college girls there. Plus, a warm day on the coast of Maine was marvelous. That might have been my best summer ever.

A year later, I was not such a priapic all-star at the Monmouth Hotel, perhaps because I was nervous about the draft. Healthy college men did not last more than a few months after graduation before being called by the army. And in 1967, they needed troops.

Most soldiers who went to Vietnam, of course, were not killed. Or even wounded. But I was not a bellicose young man. I had never even been in a fistfight. The army benefited from my absence.

In late July 1967, I was drinking with my college buddies almost every night as my agitation grew. But this social loitering proved to be effective.

I was in bed on a Friday, about 11 a.m. after bar hopping in New York City, when my mother, Eloise, took a call from Washington, D.C. If my father, a business exec who ground out a commute to Manhattan every day, had known I was sleeping until almost noon, he would have been displeased. But my mother rolled with it. She got me out of bed—without judgment—for the call.

It was the VISTA Volunteer HR department in D.C. The caller had two programs to offer. But I had to leave in two days. "Where are the programs?" I asked. "One is in Watts," she replied. Watts was in Los Angeles, and it was still smoldering from civil insurrection. "And the other?" I asked. "Honolulu."

The term "no-brainer" is overused. But it seems to fit here. I was thrilled. "I'll want to talk with my parents," I said, a sign of a young guy whose parents were still paying the bills. The caller replied, "You have an hour. We're filling both programs today." Click. Seconds later, my mother got the news. She smiled. "Sounds good," she said. "You might want to call your father."

My father, Clint, had served in the army (stateside) during World War II. He even brought home memorabilia. Some came back with a German helmet or a Japanese bayonet. He brought back bunk beds with the U.S. imprimatur on the wood. He got them while in Indiana.

My father expected me to go into the army. Many parents in mid-1967 still did. My father was an accountant-type and not a sympathetic mentor. Even though the son of one of his office colleagues had been killed in Vietnam the previous year, my father still thought I should join. Not that he had risked his life in the trenches. Clint Hendrickson was a great tennis player. In later years, I learned that much of his army time was spent giving tennis exhibitions for the troops.

He picked up the phone in his Manhattan office. He seemed surprised that I was joining VISTA, which suggested he had not listened very closely when I was discussing career plans. He did not give his blessing, but he assented.

Descriptions of me then would have included "laconic" and "low-key." But on this July day, the descriptive term would have been "ebullient." Think of a giddier-than-usual Robin Williams.

The call was returned to VISTA staffers. I would take Honolulu. My HR contact in Washington seemed to chuckle. "You got the last slot for Hawaii," she said. "The next selectee is going to Watts."

Acceptance to VISTA on a sleepy Friday was a lucky break, my 1-A alternative. From a nervous countdown to Vietnam, my mental gymnastics now involved plans to go to Honolulu.

A journey to fight poverty in the Pacific was certainly a new direction for a Hendrickson. My parents had come from mainstream Republicans.

My father was the last of seven children of Ralph and Phoebe Hendrickson, of Bellerose, Long Island. The Hendricksons had arrived in 1682 and reportedly received a grant from fellow Dutchman Peter Stuyvesant. The modern Hendricksons were wealthy during the Depression, owning a car, a truck and a 100-acre farm near the border of Brooklyn.

My mother, Eloise Carter, was an only child who was born in North Carolina. Her mother, Edith Carter, left her husband in Winston-Salem, N.C., when Edith was about twenty. Edith and Eloise traveled to New York City, where Edith, later to be known as Gia, started a career as a shop girl. She was later a high-end buyer of ladies' coats and suits, a self-made woman who helped our family greatly.

Despite the depression, both of my parents graduated from college in 1940. My father went to Gettysburg College. My mother went to Douglas (Rutgers) and transferred to Hood College in Frederick, Maryland. They were married in 1940. My mother died in 1974, and my father passed in 1992.

My sister, Dale, born in 1943, also went to Gettysburg. She was a teacher in Ann Arbor, Michigan, and is now retired. She has been a terrific, loving sibling.

Some writers claim they were formed by personal misfortune or an unstable family. But no abuse, desertion or lack of opportunity can be found in my background. In my early years, a loving family and a lot of luck helped get me started.

4

Fighting Poverty

When I graduated in 1967, I was accepted as a VISTA Volunteer. VISTA was an altruistic organization like the Peace Corp. Many Volunteers worked in tough urban neighborhoods or distant retreats with Native Americans. I was sent to Hawaii. A small volume could be written about this meaningful and educational experience. Perhaps another time.

5

Next Stop: Grad School in Berkeley

Toward the end of a two-year stay, I had to make a decision on the next move. I had already extended the VISTA tenure by a year and had to leave the program after the tenure of 1967–69.

The Vietnam War was still raging. The draft boards were still reaching out for bodies.

It might seem odd today that the Vietnam War played such a large role in the lives of youthful Americans, but probably 80 percent of young men faced military service. They did not all go, of course, but media coverage of the Vietnam War brought the fighting home.

Hundreds of Americans were dying each month. Thousands of Vietnamese were losing their lives. At one point the U.S. was "carpet-bombing" portions of that country, and it will never be known how many Asians died.

Because of its location in the Pacific, the war was very visible in Hawaii.

After the Tet Offensive in the winter of 1968, nearby Tripler Military Hospital overflowed with wounded soldiers flown in from Saigon. Many Halawa residents were part of emergency teams. They worked overtime as nurses, medical assistants and military drivers to accommodate the wounded.

During my tenure, the civilian airport in Honolulu was full of military personnel. Some had landed with their units to refuel on their way to Vietnam. Others, already serving, took their R and R (rest and recuperation) in Honolulu. Stories in local media reflected the anguish of the young men who were spending a week in paradise before returning to the hell of battle. Military statistics show that 58,000 Americans were killed and perhaps 600,000 wounded. In later years, many more soldiers would evince signs of post-war trauma and mental instability.

Deferments were being granted to those who attended theological seminary. A lapsed Lutheran, I applied to a seminary in Berkeley, Calif. I was accepted.

The Pacific Lutheran Theological Seminary was in the spectacular Berkeley Hills. The view of the bay and San Francisco behind it was breathtaking. A quick bus ride down the winding hills put you on the exciting UC campus.

Classes about biblical history and clerical activism were interesting. But I had no money. Several jobs helped: a part-time bagger post at Lucky's Supermarket and a part-time waiter gig at the Claremont Hotel in Berkeley. There was a freelance writer's job for a new magazine, Atlantis.

During that fall, there was a seismic shift in the lives of draft-eligible American men. In late November 1969, the Selective Service Commission held a lottery to determine which young men would be taken into the military. This move by the Nixon Administration was taken to end the relentless protesting that was enveloping campuses and many cities. Nixon believed that if half of the eligible men were suddenly ineligible, the protests would diminish. And that is what happened.

On the day of the public drawing of lottery numbers, my number was a glorious 309. Selective Service officials suggested that a youth with that high a number would not be touched. My new life now included options. Newspaper jobs could be sought. I could get married.

The young woman making the dubious commitment to me was Vicki Lawson, a pretty native of Memphis who had gone to Mississippi State College for Women. We had met at the Samoset Hotel in Rockland, Maine, in 1966. She had come to visit in Hawaii. She and I spent the summer of 1969 in Maine, and then we drove to her home in Memphis to announce the news.

We went to Maine in 1969 because I had purchased land there the year before. In 1968, *The Saturday Review of Books* (long defunct) had a classified section, and an ad announced, "Land in Maine, $25 per acre."

There were no single one-acre parcels for $25, of course. But available was some land on the Sandy River in a small town (New Sharon) near Farmington. This area is about ninety minutes northwest of Portland. My grandmother, "Gia," helped with the down payment. The owner, Charles Sewall, of Bath, Maine, agreed to take a note. For the next two years, he was paid $40 per month. Eventually the sum of about $3,000 was paid.

That said, owning 18 acres on the unmighty Sandy has been thrilling. We have put a cabin on it, with a wood stove in the corner of the 20-by-20-foot structure. In the front yard, there is a well with wonderful drinking water. It is one of the few investments that worked out. In 2021, I gave it to our children, Leslie and Drew. The real estate attorney, a friend named Paul Mills (brother of Gov. Janet Mills), put a clause in the agreement that declares I can never be evicted if I visit.

But getting back to marriage. In 1969, Vicki and I headed from Rockland, Maine, to Memphis to meet her folks. Her mother, Virginia King Lawson, was wonderful. Her father, Weston G. Lawson, was an unpleasant, would-be patriarch. They had been divorced for years, but he was still on the scene.

W. G. was a horse trader. The day after we arrived in Memphis, he went out of his way to make me look foolish before a group of horse owners at his farm.

The following is an essay I wrote in December 2019, to mark our 50th anniversary. Some of this prose repeats information already shared, but it is informative of the first years together:

It is our 50th anniversary and this essay is a remembrance of that wedding day five decades ago.

The times were turbulent. The Vietnam War was its peak and many men my age were getting drafted. The threat of injury or death was substantial.

Because of the war, most of my college friends were scattered. They could not attend our wedding in Memphis.

Some had been nabbed by the Army and were overseas; others were avoiding the draft and were keeping a low profile. I didn't know where they were.

Only a few of my friends were able to attend. My parents, Eloise and Clint Hendrickson, came, as did my grandmother, Edith Carter, and my aunt, Beatrice Hostetter, of Glen Head, Long Island.

My sister, Dale, could not travel because she had just given birth to a daughter, Dara, in Ann Arbor, Michigan.

Vicki's girlfriends from Memphis and the W attended.

I was living in Berkeley, Calif., in December of 1969, and I was nervous flying into Memphis for the wedding. I had met W.G.—Vicki's father—that fall after we drove in from Rockland, Maine.

W.G., a horse trader, wasn't friendly to me. He termed me the "Yankee joker" and in September he made fun of me at his farm by having me walk a frisky horse in front of a crowd of horse owners. The horse reared. I could not control him. As he planned, I looked like a fool in front of many horse-savvy guests.

Vicki's mother, Virginia, was wonderful. But in the days before the wedding, she was in a flux because there had been a fire in her apartment. Her unit wasn't ruined but clothes had to be cleaned and the living area had to be scrubbed. Her neighbor across the hall—gone for the holiday—permitted us to use his residence.

I didn't want a wedding cake, and I didn't want her brothers, Bobby and Wes, to tie cans to the back of the car, a white '63 Corvair, as was done at the time. I was uptight, as we used to say.

We got married in a chateau owned by a friend of Virginia. We prevailed upon Vicki to dress at the chateau. We were concerned that Vicki might be tardy. Even back in 1969, the word was out that she was generally late.

Vicki employed a wonderful harp player, and she and her mother arranged everything.

We had Virginia's minister declare us "man and wife." The ceremony was in front of a large Christmas tree and took about 20 minutes. Aunt Bea said it was the strangest wedding she had ever attended.

One of the readings was from Beatitudes, which was the basis for a popular song suggesting that "For Everything There Is a Season." We have had many wonderful seasons since 1969.

We did not rent the local Elks that night. The reception was back at the fire-prone apartment, and it was terrific once the booze arrived.

Virginia had aggregated several bottles of wine, but her inventory was not nearly enough for the Hendrickson crowd. Generous Uncle Bobby went out for beer, wine and whiskey and his timely trip enabled joyous moments to unfold.

Vicki and I went to a nearby hotel the first night, and we were quite thrilled with ourselves. We stayed in town for a few days after the nuptials, which was unusual for the time.

Regarding our loitering, we had some figuring to do.

We needed jobs. In California, we knew no one. But we had confidence born out of ignorance. Vicki was an optimist. And we were both dreamers.

So, after the unpretentious but wonderful wedding, we headed west.

I started writing stories on a freelance basis. And I was applying for positions in the newspaper field.

Vicki got a job at the local Bank of America in Oakland. We were in the Fruitvale section. It was a very dangerous neighborhood. She vowed she would give away the bank's money if any of the hard cases decided to knock over the branch (as armed heiress Patty Hearst would do later that year in another part of the Bay Area).

Vicki wasn't robbed. But our supermarket across the street was. After gallantly walking her to her job one morning, I stopped to see why so many Oakland cop cars had converged with lights flashing. It turns out an armed robber had tried to stick up the place. Things went wrong and he took hostages.

But he lost his cool—or perhaps he gained it—when he took several employees into the meat freezer as hostages. His first demand was hot coffee. His second demand was for heavy coats.

The police got him coffee. And then they just waited. The disconsolate robber emerged—teeth chattering—after about an hour and he was arrested. There were no injuries.

Our life in Oakland didn't last long, because I got a reporter's job in Petaluma, about 40 miles north of San Francisco. This was one of my major breaks in journalism.

I had submitted applications to every news organization in northern California, and I got a bite with the *Argus-Courier* in Petaluma.

At the interview, I asked for $90 per week. Evidently seeing great promise, the publisher offered me $115 per week—and I took it. I was thrilled. It was another Robin Williams moment—exuberance.

We settled in a modest little white house, three miles into the country. Vicki took art classes at the local community college and won a cash award.

I covered the City Council and the police department, and with overtime I sometimes made $160 per week. We didn't complain.

Petaluma was one of the fastest growing communities in the country, and litigation involving the city's moratorium on residential building went to the U.S. Supreme Court.

> There was an enormous national story a few towns away. Black Panthers broke into a federal courthouse and freed a half-dozen convicts who were being tried. They kidnapped a judge, and the judge and several jurors were killed in the getaway. Several convicts also died in the blaze of gunfire that broke out. I wrote second-day stories on several of the journalists, hostages and guards involved. Angela Davis was a key figure in the invasion.
>
> I had arrived. Big stories and an exciting future.

Now, in 2025, it is almost unimaginable that Vicki and I took such risks half a continent away from our families and friends. We knew no one in Petaluma when we arrived.

6

An Introvert's Newspaper Career Begins

The career began in 1970. Journalism was a good choice. I liked to read and enjoyed processing new information.

An introvert, I did not mind standing in the back of the room and listening. I was thrilled by big events, but I was not forceful enough to make news myself. My career was following the events that others created.

And newspapers were successful from 1970 through about 2000. The whole economy was.

Baby boomers have lived through a prosperous era. A lot went right for middle-class Americans during this period. My parents and teachers said that our generation (born 1940 to 1960) was the most blessed of any. Our elders had come out of the depression and World War II. Their children had many opportunities.

For instance, in the late '60s and '70s, there were jobs. When liberal arts majors were getting into the workforce, huge social programs were being launched.

The War on Poverty was started by President Lyndon Johnson in the mid-'60s. Thousands of new positions were created in a drive to improve education and health. Community Action Programs hired personnel around the clock.

In a related development, the Environmental Protection Agency was launched in 1970. More than 1,000 jobs were filled in the first year, and it kept growing at both the federal and state levels. NASA and other federal programs were also getting off the ground.

In addition, big companies were hiring. Enterprises trained young recruits. The '50s, '60s, and '70s were boom times for many parts of the U.S. economy.

There were tough times following World War II, of course. The civil rights movement of the late '50s and early '60s highlighted inequity and produced violent and distasteful moments. The Vietnam War was a nightmare for hundreds of thousands of Americans—and millions of Vietnamese. The AIDS epidemic shattered the lives of an uncountable number of families starting in the '80s.

Yet the post-war era provided opportunities to many (white) Americans. Virtually all of my adult life was spent in the media business—with a press pass. My life was my lifestyle.

The early years in print were exciting. Newspapers were flush with cash, and energetic editors were chasing the next big story. After the turn of the century (2000), I barely managed to hang on. Many newspapers did not.

There were many setbacks in this long career. Jobs were lost, and sometimes our little family had to move to find work in the newspaper field. But we prevailed.

7

Reporter's Job in Petaluma, Calif.

If being accepted to VISTA and getting a high lottery number were Big Breaks No. 1 and No. 2, landing a job on the *Argus-Courier* was Big Break No. 3.

Publisher Ross Game of the Scripps League hired me on February 13, 1970. My beat was city hall and the police, plus I would write feature stories. Vicki would be an artist. She took free art courses with a neighbor at a local junior college, and she joined the Newcomers' Club.

The job of municipal reporter was great. The editors and other reporters were very patient. I had very little writing experience. I had been the editor of my high school newspaper and a sports stringer for a handful of newspapers in northern Jersey. And I had written a few stories for the college newspaper and yearbook. I had never been inside a city hall, anywhere. The bottom line was that I was green.

In this fast-growing city, a confrontation arose between builders and real estate interests and residents who didn't stand to make money. The developers were winning. The mayor was Helen Putnam, a septuagenarian, a long-time resident, and a thoughtful leader. She declared that the sewage treatment plant had to be expanded before more houses could be approved. This was her tactic to slow down rampant building.

The debate took two years, and eventually it went to the U.S. Supreme Court. The court ruled that communities have the right to regulate growth, even if development companies own land and qualify for permits.

There must have been fifty meetings and forums. We had an afternoon newspaper, meaning we wrote our stories in the morning. The paper came out at about 2 p.m. I quickly caught on to the routine and became a valuable member of our ten-person editorial team.

While local political issues were taking up much time, a fun event was the World Wrist-Wrestling Championships. An *Argus-Courier* columnist, Bill Soberanes, ran a wrist-twisting session at a local bar. He expanded it to the local armory. And then he was able to sell it to ABC's "Wide World of Sports." Hundreds of matches took place at the local armory, and fans screamed for their favorites. It sounds simple, but ABC-TV was able to breathe life into an event that occurs in every tavern in the country.

Vicki and I went to our first press party. Free food. Free drinks. The press pass made it possible.

For a young reporter of twenty-four who was looking for excitement, Petaluma was a happening place. Politicians frequently stopped in Petaluma and visited our newspaper. We had ten writers and/or photographers. Circulation was about 8,000.

Sen. John Tunney dropped in, and he and I took a ride from Petaluma to Santa Rosa, his next campaign stop. On another occasion, Republican Ronald Reagan stopped by to seek the endorsement of the Scripps League (twenty-six newspapers). Reagan served as governor from 1972 to 1980, and as president from 1980 to 1988.

On a self-assigned trip to San Francisco, I was in the same elevator with San Francisco Mayor Joseph Alioto and New York Mayor John Lindsay. They answered my hurried questions about the future of urban centers. The city hall reporter for a small newspaper did not have to attend a national meeting of the country's urban mayors. But if you had energy and ambition, there were a lot of stories to chase.

One night Vicki and I went to the Press Club in San Francisco for a meeting of Sigma Delta Chi, the Professional Journalism Society. Many correspondents who were covering the Vietnam War stopped here. Delivering tales of coverage and warfare were reporters such as Peter Arnett of the Associated Press and Horst Fass, a prominent free-lance photographer.

Vicki, pretty and vivacious, danced with Paul Finch, the AP Bureau chief in Mexico City. I would later get a recommendation from him that enabled me to join the Mexico City *News*.

On a small publication like the *Argus-Courier*, one could just about choose your stories. Our editor, Ralph Thompson, and our reporter, AP veteran Del Miller, were generous in their praise and thoughtful about criticism.

Reporters carried Pentax cameras and, of course, handed over film to be developed.

Our editor overlooked mistakes. In one edition I had a story asserting that the Shell Oil Co. in Petaluma was polluting local waterways. Actually, it was the tiny Petaluma Shell Co. that was under investigation, not the mammoth petroleum company (which had a small office nearby). The editor and I sat down with several annoyed executives from Shell Oil's PR team. A correction was written, which is an exercise that journalists hate to undertake.

I was very thin-skinned; I shied away from controversial stories. Because of my aversion to criticism, jobs I sought in the future would include posts that called for feature stories, not hard news.

Positions in the future would include sportswriter, news writer, entertainment editor, lifestyle columnist, book reviewer, waterfront reporter and technology correspondent. Late in my career, I became a writer of regional maritime books.

Reporter's Job in Petaluma, Calif.

Investigative newsmen like David Halberstam, Neil Sheehan, Bob Woodward, and Carl Bernstein were in vogue in the '70s. But in a placid farming community like Petaluma, there was not much mayhem to cover.

One profile I wrote was on an unknown local musician named Norman Greenbaum. His young manager set up an interview, and Norman came strolling into the newsroom with a guitar and a grin. The manager had not briefed me; I had not done much research. But Norman had written and sung a song titled "Spirit in the Sky."

Several months later it emerged as an enormous national hit. Fifty years later, it is still heard on the radio. My amateurish questions to Norman included, "How is the single doing?" "How is the album doing?" "How is the tour doing?"

The *Argus-Courier* was the first media stop for the singer. But there is no joke here. The interview with Dyke Hendrickson was one of the first media appearances on Greenbaum's long and very successful career.

A more serious writing project was a story of a proposed dredging operation in nearby Jenner. An excavation company wanted to take gravel from the Russian River. The well-paid lawyers for the dredging company quietly argued that industry needed gravel to build roads and bridges. But there was vigorous opposition. Poorly dressed activists screamed at county commissioners that a precious natural river that was home to fish, birds and other wildlife should not be ruined by greed. Several angry dissidents were escorted from the hearing by local sheriffs.

The governmental drama involving a valuable resource was riveting. And it ended well, at least for the moment. No dredging.

In other assignments, interviews included political candidates, Chamber of Commerce leaders, moguls of fish farming and even a few Jesus freaks.

Our recreational trips included jaunts to Bodega Bay, Lake Tahoe, Mendocino, Sacramento, and Point Reyes. Those months in Petaluma were fun.

8

Selling Everything and Moving to Mexico

Despite living a fine life, Vicki and I decided to move to Mexico. Most people go on vacations. In our early life, we moved.

I wanted to be a foreign correspondent, just like the AP's Peter Arnett. Vicki liked adventure. So we began looking at maps and figuring how we would decamp for Mexico.

I gave notice of leaving after about eighteen months. Our peers were surprised; the "adults" in the newsroom and in the community were baffled. But we sold everything, including our albums, artwork, and the Corvair ($150), and boarded a bus for Mazatlán on the west coast.

We had no jobs in Mexico. We knew no one in the entire country. But I did have a letter of recommendation from the AP's Paul Finch, whom Vicki had dazzled on the dance floor.

Several dozen Petalumans saw us off at the bus station. Vicki was tardy, but they held the bus until she arrived. She was late because she had been mailing her valuable wedding rings back to her mother in Memphis so they would not be lost or stolen.

When we departed, we had $600 in traveler checks. What a paltry sum with which to start a new life! In another country! She carried a small suitcase, and a large box of paints and canvases. I lugged a suitcase and a typewriter. This was Jack Kerouac material, south of the border. But we weren't "lost." I was going to be a writer; Vicki was going to be an artist and free spirit.

Mexico was beautiful and fascinating, especially from the window of a bus. The colorful vistas across desert ranges and anonymous mountain ranges were exquisite.

Contemplating the lives of random residents in the area was fascinating. Our bus would have driven for two hours in a desolate desert, when we would see a family with small pieces of luggage walking along the road. Not even a bicycle was in sight. We cruised for two hours more before getting to a small village. We asked ourselves, where was this family going? How did they live?

The golds, oranges, and browns of the landscape were breathtaking. The scrub vegetation made us wish we had brought a few books to help explain this exotic region. Texas had been scenic but there were oil wells, small towns and national chain rest stops to remind one that this was the good old USA. One drove for hours in western Mexico seeing only long stretches of sand, stone, and dust.

The city of Mazatlán was our first destination. When the bus finally stopped, Vicki's box of art supplies fell on the head of the pleasant middle-aged Mexican woman in front of us. She was uninjured. But gracious. In fact, every Mexican citizen we met was cordial and helpful. This was a departure from stereotypes of many U.S. movies, that Mexicans were lazy and even resentful of American tourists. The residents we met were great.

We arrived at our hotel in Mazatlán about 9 a.m. We sat down for breakfast in the modest hotel with the woman whose cranium had been dented by Vicki's sturdy box of paints. She ordered a beer. "You can never tell about the drinking water," she said.

A beer at 9 a.m.? On advice from a native? That works. After several brews and a tasty meal of ranchos huevos, we got into our fan-conditioned room and slept off our "bus lag."

That evening, we were transfixed by the beauty of the Pacific. With the enormous sun setting in the crimson west, it was spectacular. An older gentleman, Alberto de Campos, joined us for a drink at the hotel and asked us if we wanted to take a ride in a horse and buggy he had reserved. We were young. We believed in people. "Sure."

The ride was slow and spectacular, as we viewed the setting sun. The orange of the sky turned to red, and then a spectacular purple. Our host bought a tray of pajaritos from a street vendor. These are tiny fish, cooked in tasty sauces. They were delicious.

From the newsboys on the street to the real estate middlemen who helped us find an apartment, everyone we met was cordial. I never saw a fistfight or heard an angry word. Nothing went wrong.

We stayed for a day or two. And then we remembered we had a mission. So we boarded a bus for San Miguel de Allende, in the central mountains.

San Miguel is a gringo destination. Yet having English-speaking residents around would be helpful. I was going to write a novel. If not that, I had to earn some language creds so I could emerge as a foreign correspondent. Vicki loved art and there was plenty of that in San Miguel.

We knew no one in San Miguel. But upon arriving my faulty Spanish enabled us to learn that there was a garden apartment available for about $60 a month. We took it.

San Miguel is built upon the American tourist trade. Also, many Americans retire there. There are several schools offering classes, from silver design to revolutionary history of Mexico. Vicki signed up for art. I enrolled in advanced Spanish (for gringos). We found a pool that was chlorinated. We wrote letters to our parents that indicated that we had arrived and were in a "learning mode."

I began to plan "my novel." One reason for leaving the 8-to-5 regimen of newspaper work was to write fiction. This is a daydream of many journalists. The problem was, I had no story in my mind.

Many accomplished writers, from Stephen King to Tess Gerritsen, have said that the writer really needs an idea, characters, a plot, and personal drive.

I had a daydream but no story. I hadn't lived enough; I didn't know enough. I would sit in our garden apartment, but no words filled the page. Vicki would return from art class, but I had few words to show her. I could procrastinate. I could sip Oso Negro vodka. I just couldn't get the novel moving.

As I later learned, our parents could not comprehend what we were doing. We had left a stable work-life situation in comfortable northern California and had bolted to unpredictable Mexico. Why? The same question began to occur to us.

After several weeks in San Miguel, we were losing yardage. We were studying with interesting people; we were eating fine food in inexpensive restaurants. We were having fun in a foreign land. But our $600 was disappearing.

So I stepped up as a provider. I applied for a job at the Mexico City *News*, an English language newspaper. It is difficult for an American to get a job in Mexico because officials want to provide jobs for their own residents.

But Vicki's buddy Paul Finch from the Mexico City AP had written a letter of recommendation to the editor, Jaime Plenn. It proved to be crucial. The bus ride to Mexico City was three hours. Mr. Plenn interviewed me. And then he hired me as a copy editor. I would edit stories, write captions and propose headlines. I would also translate press releases.

Vicki, back in San Miguel, was elated when she learned the news. She was, and is, an energetic supporter. And she loves adventures. After finishing our courses, we headed toward the big city. It was enormous. And in parts, incredibly poor. We stayed in the Pink (Rosa) Zone, which meant a comfortable neighborhood with numerous Americans.

My shift at the newspaper was 3 p.m. to 10 p.m. That left Vicki alone for much of the day. As a blonde, blue-eyed, pretty young woman, she was harassed on the street by young men doing their machismo harassment. She could not go anywhere in public without being followed. And because she knew no one in the city, she could not get a friend to accompany her.

Also, we had our cash flow problem. My job paid $7 a day. The room at the Geneve Hotel cost $8. And since we had only a few hundred dollars left, we were heading for trouble.

Mexico was not working. After a few weeks, we made plans to go home.

This failure to launch created great angst. I second-guessed the decision to leave California. Couldn't we just have vacationed in Mexico?

The answer was, we didn't want to settle in California. It was too far from our families. And we thought things would always get better.

But as the bard says, youth shouldn't be wasted on the young. We had impulsively gone south. The trip had been exciting. We had traveled to cities including Acapulco, Guadalajara, Guanajuato, Mazatlán, and Mexico City. Vicki had enjoyed her art studies in San Miguel; my Spanish improved.

But as the summer of 1971 ended, we were out of money. And we had no car.

We took a bus to Memphis, Vicki's hometown. We stayed there for several weeks while I applied for newspaper jobs with the local papers, *The Commercial-Appeal* and the *Memphis Press Scimitar*. Vicki's mother, Virginia Lawson, a medical professional in diabetic research, was hoping we would settle nearby. But there were no positions available.

What next? Maine, of course.

9

Another Great Break: A Job in Portland, Maine

My grandmother, Gia, gave us a car. It was a '65 Corvair, two years "newer" than the beat-up vehicle we sold in Petaluma. The new ride enabled us to travel to New England. We were jobless, homeless, and carless in Memphis, but we did have land in Maine. We decided to head for the Pine Tree State.

Maine is beautiful in summer. And there were those 18 acres on the Sandy River in central Maine, in New Sharon, and it was near the state capital, Augusta. We would camp; we would revel in nature; we would look for jobs. Our tent was 17 feet long and 10 feet wide. Vicki once cooked a three-course meal in the tent, including gravy for the fried chicken.

But obstacles emerged. When we camped on the land, our car got stuck in the mud. Swarms of mosquitoes attacked. And the parcel was so large (600 yards to the river), we couldn't find the Sandy in which to bathe and clean up.

It wasn't long before we realized we couldn't live in a cloth tent through a Maine winter. Next move: job search. I wrote to all the newspapers in the region.

Our good fortune held. The *Biddeford-Saco Journal* hired me in October 1971. Biddeford was a mill town on the Saco River in southern Maine. But like many New England communities, it had lost its mills when anti-union owners moved to the South. The city was dreary; it was dirty. But its newspaper offered a full-time perch as a city hall reporter and a sportswriter. That newspaper, which had a circulation of 10,000, folded in 2019. But it gave us life at the time.

This was another enormous break—a full-time job with benefits in a community on the scenic Saco River and near the Atlantic Ocean.

In later life, it became difficult to find jobs and settle into communities. But at this point I had good clips from *The Argus-Courier*, and I conveyed enthusiasm. In September 1971, I started at the *Journal* at $150 per week. And I got overtime covering sports on weekends. My background as a high-school stringer in New Jersey was helpful here.

I had the confidence that I could do a good job as a city hall reporter during the week and a sportswriter on the weekends. In this pre-Watergate era, there weren't as many journalists out there.

In 2025, I am astonished at the risks we took.

If landing a full-time job in a new community was not enough good fortune, Vicki found us a small cottage at Fortunes Rocks Beach in coastal Biddeford Pool. The two-bedroom retreat overlooked a fresh-water pond. Beyond that was a glorious view of the Atlantic, impeded only by a few handsome summer homes.

The rental fee was incredibly low: $80 per month. When friends visited, they could not believe that was the price. But it was owned by a Dr. Gordon Adamson, an eighty-five-year-old, retired Unitarian minister who lived next door. He wanted credible tenants who would not give him trouble. Vicki closed the deal on this one.

Several weeks later, Vicki got a part-time job at the Unitarian Church. Soon after, she landed a full-time job as a teacher's assistant in the Saco school system.

What good luck. What good fortune. We had taken an enormous risk by leaving California with no credible plan. Yet we surfaced on the Atlantic coast with two jobs and a seaside cottage for small money.

We would not always be so lucky. In 1976, our first child died. But in late 1971, our adventure was continuing.

In 1973, I was hired by the *Portland Press Herald* as a district correspondent covering Biddeford, Saco and Kennebunk. The *Press Herald* was the largest newspaper in southern Maine (circulation 55,000). Its weekend edition, *The Maine Sunday Telegram*, was the largest in the state (circulation 115,000). Talking about numbers, my salary rose from about $150 per week to about $400 per week.

One of my jobs as bureau chief of the York County bureau in Biddeford was to cover city council meetings. Stories were produced on the selectmen of Kennebunk and Kennebunkport. The city councils of Biddeford and Saco were covered. There was very little crime to cover in these small communities.

Biddeford and Saco were mill cities, each about 15,000 in population. They were characterized by enormous brick mill buildings that lined the streets of the downtowns. Textile mills of the nineteenth century were on almost every river in Maine.

The Industrial Revolution started in Lowell, Massachusetts, in the 1820s. Inventors learned how to harness the power of fast-moving rivers to power mill machinery. Lowell and Lawrence were actually the Silicon Valley of the day, meaning this new technology was powering profitable industries like the manufacture of cotton, wool and shoes.

Mills came to almost every Maine riverside community in the nineteenth century. Jobs were plentiful. Communities like Biddeford and Saco welcomed immigrants from nearby Quebec to work in these huge manufacturing buildings.

Women were hired with enthusiasm and some mills created day-care centers for moms who brought their kids to work. Stores thrived in the downtowns of these mill cities, because in the late nineteenth century and early twentieth century, few workers had cars.

In southern New England, many mill workers were Irish, Italian, or eastern European. In Maine communities, most workers were French speakers from Quebec. When we moved to Biddeford in the early '70s, locals spoke French on the streets.

We were amazed by how large the buildings were in Biddeford. They were mostly empty by this time, but it was a culture shock to see the entire downtown blanketed by lengthy brick structures.

Meanwhile, we were living on the ocean in Fortunes Rocks. We never had such a picturesque little home, with birds aplenty and just a 100-yard walk to the Atlantic.

One of the most intriguing stories at the time developed when Biddeford Mayor Gilbert Boucher suddenly announced that the city was taking by eminent domain several acres on the Atlantic for a public park. The acreage was owned by a wealthy private beach club, composed of owners of enormous summer homes who lived in Boston, New York and Washington.

These club members were shocked. Who were these upstart city councilors taking away their gorgeous waterfront? Mayor Boucher, the blunt-talking son of mill workers, said that hard-working people of the city deserved a beach. At the time, there was no public park on the ocean at which residents could swim, picnic and walk the beach.

The wealthy summer homeowners fought the takeover. But the courts eventually sided with the city. Biddeford had to pay for the land, but Mayor Boucher had struck a blow for the descendants of families who had powered the mills. The beach is still used today, and there is a plaque honoring the history-conscious mayor. Boucher, a non-drinking building contractor, died at fifty-five.

After covering the local communities, I started looking for other things to do.

One of my most enjoyable forays in obtaining "media access" was attending the Kentucky Derby in 1973. That was the year the fabled Secretariat won. Because I had wangled an "all-access" press pass, I was in the pricey box seats adjacent to the finish line when the great horse thundered to victory.

The backstory: I was working for the *Press Herald* and about to fly to Memphis to join Vicki and her family. I noticed that the Derby was being run that weekend in Louisville, Kentucky, and I called the press office at the racetrack to ask for a press pass.

The media director, Raymond Johnson, had not heard of me. I am not sure he had heard of Portland, Maine. But he was a very nice guy. "I can't get you a seat in the press box. It's full. But I'll leave a press badge at the Will Call window." Good enough.

I hopped on a plane from Portland and rented a car at the Louisville airport, which must have been the last vehicle left on this busy weekend. My press pass enabled me to enter the first-class section adjacent to the track, and this vantage point was actually better than sitting in a press box high above the finish line.

It was thrilling to see such an exciting race among a fervent crowd. This race draws a drinking crowd. And perhaps because it is in the South, the women get all gussied up, with colorful, full dresses and enormous wide-brimmed hats. The Kentucky Derby itself was one of the last races of a long day. Spectators were partially drunk but very friendly. Even those who tore up their losing tickets seemed to be enjoying the sunny day.

Later, I slept in the car at the airport. When I finally got to the family gathering in Memphis, I had plenty to talk about. I never wrote a story about the event. It seemed too unbelievable, not to say unprofessional, to write a story about this impulsive adventure.

In 1974, I was promoted to work in Portland as a sportswriter. This was a dream job. Bob Moorehead, about thirty-five at the time, was the sports editor. One reason for my quick ascension in the sports department was tennis. I covered tennis for the *Press Herald* during the "Tennis Boom." And as an energetic twenty-something, I expanded my domain so I could cover the national championships at Forest Hills.

The newspaper picked up some bills, but now I did not have to take refuge in a rented car. I stayed with my parents in Demarest, N.J., or with my aunt, Beatrice Hostetter, in Glen Head, on Long Island.

In 1974, I managed to obtain credentials to Wimbledon. That was the year that Jimmy Connors and Chris Evert were crowned champions—the "Love Double," as it was dubbed. Connors and Chrissie were engaged, though she used her good sense to dump the irascible Connors. Their presence drew enormous media attention. Also in the news was Billie Jean King, who fessed up to having an abortion not long before.

It was unusual for a young sportswriter from a small market like Portland to cover Wimbledon, but Bob Moorehead was one of the few editors who was happy to encourage his writers if the coverage would bring a new dimension to the newspaper. *The Maine Sunday Telegram* ran promotional stories before the coverage. Newspapers are not good at self-promotion, but Moorehead had his own style.

At Wimbledon, there was no press pass. The media manager at the All-England Club did not have me on the list. This was his mistake, because I had the credentials letter somewhere in my luggage.

I was arguing with the media liaison when tennis icon Bud Collins of *The Boston Globe* walked by. "Wait, he's OK," chirped Bud. "He's from Portland, Maine, and he covers Forest Hills every year." Newspaper professionals are famously reticent and often unfriendly, but Bud was a gregarious exception.

Vicki and I stayed with a couple, Nell and Ken Bowker, in Surrey. They were peers of my parents. Vicki went sightseeing during the day with Nell. I covered the matches by day. Stories were cabled back to the newspaper, and I sent film by mail. At night, I drank beer with Ken. I was able to get Ken a temporary pass to the Wimbledon final between Connors and veteran Ken Rosewall.

In the press room, I held Chris Evert's hand and admired her engagement ring, which Jimmy had given her. It was a solitaire. Vicki wore a solitaire, a hand-off from my benevolent grandmother, Gia. Chris and I were both naïve. A solitaire is only a style, as in single stone. Somehow, I thought it was a high-end designer product. She thanked me for my interest. Chris was a taciturn teen. On the court, she was a quiet but resolute competitor. She rarely made unforced errors, and she was great under pressure. Now a popular TV commentator, Chrissie remains one of the most popular of U.S. champions. She was married to three handsome athletes: tennis player John Lloyd, skier Andy Mill, and golfer Greg Norman. All three ended in divorce.

Host Ken Bowker recalled he had taken shooting practice on the Wimbledon grounds during World War II. On that theme, Rosewall must have felt like he was the target of gunfire that day, because Connors blasted him 6-1, 6-0, 6-1.

With press credentials, Vicki and I went to the Wimbledon Ball at the Grosvenor Hotel. As winners, Chris, nineteen, and Jimmy, twenty-two, danced the first dance. What a thrilling night!

Our run of remarkable good fortune ended in 1973 when our first child, Vanessa, was born with a congenital heart defect. She did not come home for two weeks. She was born at Maine Medical Center in Portland and then she was taken to Children's Hospital in Boston. We were both distraught, but Vanessa lived through the first scary days. And when she was ten months old, she survived corrective surgery at Children's in Boston. But she died during a second surgery in February 1976.

Vanessa was sick but lovable. Vicki and I proceeded forth. We bought a house in Kennebunk, Maine. Vicki was working in ad sales for a television station in Portland. It was WGAN, a CBS affiliate. We attacked our careers while taking care of the vulnerable Vanessa. Vicki was very strong.

My beat expanded in the sports department. During my "off hours," I covered high school football for the newspaper. And then I launched a small video company. My video team would tape a high-school football game on Saturday and show it on local cable stations on Monday night. For instance, Portland *v.* South Portland. It was very successful. Sponsors included Coke, Kentucky Fried Chicken, and Shaw's Supermarkets. These sponsors had their own video ads, so the advertising looked professional.

I volunteered to provide coverage of the New England Patriots. This was unnecessary because the AP covered the games and provided quality photos. But it seemed like fun, so coverage started in late summer when the Patriots convened preseason training in western Massachusetts. Mixing with the players daily emphasized the size of the athletes. They were heavy and muscular, of course, but almost every athlete was about 6 feet 4 inches. And their girlfriends and wives were often over 6 feet. If they wanted a man who was taller, pro football was the place.

Tennis remained on the radar. The day that Renee Richards played in the first round of women's singles at Forest Hills in 1977 was memorable. She had once played as Dr. Richard Raskind, an eye doctor who was one of the best in the country in the thirty-five and over division. In one men's national thirty-five and over tournament at Forest Hills, he lost to tennis great Gene Scott in the semi-final round. Raskind was an excellent player.

It took enormous courage for Richard to enter the women's draw because transgender Americans were unusual at the time. Even when Olympic star Bruce Jenner changed genders decades later, there was enormous media tumult.

Richard, now Renee, was 6 feet 2 inches and had a big, lefty slice serve. When she debuted at Forest Hills, she looked so strange. Tall, broad-shouldered and with thin hair that didn't mind its manners, Renee looked bizarre on the court.

At Renee's first match, there were more media reps than at any sports event that year. TV crews arrived from Japan, radio teams from France and magazine scribes from Mexico fought for space in a crowded media center.

Renee lost in straight sets to the very capable Virginia Wade, a lithe Englishwoman who won Wimbledon a few years later. But Renee's courage in facing the media horde was admirable. She answered every question, even though it was difficult to explain some feelings in a quick TV sound bite.

Wade, a well-spoken graduate of Oxford, delivered a memorable line. Asked how she felt playing a former man, she remarked, seriously, "I hope her presence here doesn't encourage more men to change their sex so they can play in women's events."

Richards rose to become No. 23 in women's international singles rankings. She was tall and her devastating serve was the most forceful in women's tennis. She played the tournaments, and then signed to play World Team Tennis. She was an oddity, but that was fine with Billie Jean King's new WTT.

Meanwhile, Vicki was succeeding as a sales representative for WGAN-TV. The position was in Portland, and sometimes we drove the 29 miles together. We had a lovely house, with a fireplace, in comfortable Kennebunk, Maine. Life was good. Actually, it was great.

But tragedy came at the same time as did this professional advancement. Our wonderful daughter Vanessa died.

Her ailment was Ebstein's anomaly. This is a rare heart defect that's present at birth. In this condition, the tricuspid valve is in the wrong position and the valve's flaps (leaflets) are malformed. As a result, the valve does not work properly.

Many youngsters with this condition fall behind on the growth curve because their heart is not circulating an adequate amount of blood. But Vanessa was robust and had started living a normal life. Her skin was a dusky purple from lack of oxygen in her blood, and passers-by frequently warned us that our child seemed to have something wrong. We knew that very well.

Vanessa threw up often; she cried. But she was growing. She loved to smile.

Because my shift at the *Press Herald* was at night, covering late sports, my days were spent with Vanessa. We were pals.

In February 1976, she went back to Children's Hospital for what was termed as "routine corrective surgery." Our young doctor said, "On a complexity scale of 10, this is about a 3." But Vanessa, our wonderful smiling little toddler, did not survive. She died at Children's.

A memorial service was held at the Unitarian Church in Saco. Overwhelming sympathy from friends, neighbors, and work colleagues cascaded over us. Many seemed to be thinking, "Lord, I hope that never happens to my family."

This entry should be longer. But fifty years later, tears still come to my eyes.

I had lost my mother to cancer the previous year; losing my daughter brought added heartbreak.

Vicki and I cried together. We couldn't believe it. Every young couple is committed to their youngsters, and we had spent eighteen months at the side of Vanessa as the medical news seemed to get better. And then, it was over.

Vicki proved remarkably resilient. She likely cried in private as well as with me. I cried every day for months, sometimes pulling off the road because of tears.

After a celebration of life for Vanessa at the UU church, we went to Bermuda to get away from the world. But one night at a small nightclub, the well-meaning singer broke into tunes from "Sesame Street." We both started sobbing and had to leave the room. It turned out that we really couldn't get away from the world, even in pleasant Bermuda.

We went back to work. I covered high school sports, tennis and the New England Patriots football team. The drive from southern Maine to Foxboro, Mass., where the Patriots played, was about 100 miles.

The Patriots were not very good, though they had Jim Plunkett at quarterback. He had been the top collegiate player at Stanford and would later win two Super Bowls with the Oakland Raiders. Former Oklahoma coach Chuck Fairbanks was the coach. The Patriots often lost. But the adventure of covering the game, getting quotes from players, and then filing the story from the press room was an adventure for a young sportswriter.

After games, players drank beer in the locker room among the sportswriters. Several of the players smoked. How things have changed!

Vicki didn't care for her job at the TV station, but we needed two incomes. Vicki didn't find her niche until the late '90s, when she started an adult education program in Newburyport. In terms of my career, she was flexible and supportive.

Another daughter, Leslie, was born in 1976 and our son, Drew, came along in 1978. Both were healthy. We began to resume our "normal" lives following the terrible tragedy.

In terms of the sports department at the *Press Herald*, I was the only writer interested in tennis. My enthusiasm melded with the "Tennis Boom" of the '70s. And a dynamic tournament came to Maine.

In the mid-'70s, Portland hosted the Downeast Tennis Classic. Portland was a small city, with about 65,000 residents and a metro area of about 150,000. For the community to host a pro tennis tournament with some of the world's top players was an unusual development. Your Scribe covered every nanosecond.

The promoter was Gene Scott, and the years of this event were 1974–1978. Scott had been one of the best U.S. tennis players in the '60s, and after that emerged as an agent, publisher, and tournament director.

He was the grandson of Dr. Eugene Sullivan, one of the inventors of Pyrex, and Sullivan was president of Corning Glass Works. I mention the connection because Scott's inherited wealth must have been a reason why he could put on a tournament in Maine that offered enough prize money to draw top players. The event must have lost money, because the largest crowd they had was about 2,000. There was no revenue from television.

Scott chose Portland because he was chums with an influential Portland lawyer and fellow Yale grad, Harold Woodsum. Woodsum's wife, Joan, was a leader of the Portland Symphony Orchestra, which hosted the weekend event.

Scott chose early May for the eight-player singles tournament. This represented a lull between the end of the U.S. indoor season and the start of the European clay court campaign. The quality of players he recruited was amazing for a small event.

They included Ilie Nastase, then No. 2 in the world, and John McEnroe, the world's most promising junior. Other top-10ers who competed included Ken Rosewall, Vitas Gerulaitis, Dick Stockton, Cliff Drysdale, Roger Taylor, Clark Graebner, Harold Solomon, and Eddie Dibbs.

One of the tournament's most curious moments involved Rosewall. The slight Australian, thirty-nine, was one of the top players in the world. In 1974, he reached the finals of both Wimbledon and Forest Hills. He was playing Gene Mayer in the 1978 event. The young Mayer was ranked about No. 25 in the world, and he was a recent product of Stanford.

The players had split sets. As they were changing sides to begin the third set, the elderly umpire, Perry Rockafellow, descended from the chair. Rockafellow had been a nationally ranked doubles player in the '20s and coach of the Colgate men's squad for many years. Long retired at this point, he was an eccentric octogenarian.

Rosewall, as soft-spoken as they come, quietly reminded the older gentleman that there was one set remaining. Rockafellow nevertheless picked up his raincoat and umbrella and started toward the exit. "I know there is another set," he replied hurriedly to the Australian, "but if I don't leave now, I will miss the last ferry to my home on Peaks Island!"

Rosewall won, with another umpire in the chair. I suspect the well-traveled Aussie shared that tale with his cronies for many years thereafter.

Another big local event in those go-go tennis days was the Volvo International. It was played in North Conway, N.H., a small tourist village in the White Mountains of New Hampshire. It was about ninety minutes from Portland, which was one of the major markets nearby. My coverage was for a full week, with free hotel room, food, drink, and press passes.

Vicki came up to North Conway for a few days each summer, bringing the children. By 1978, we had Leslie, two, and Drew, eight weeks. We stayed at the Red Jacket Hotel that hosted the players. Arthur Ashe once passed us while we were lunching near the pool and patted tiny Drew on the head. Rod Laver shared his birthday cake with us.

Though tennis stars were lauded in those days, they were not mauled or harassed as they might be today. Ashe could read by the pool without being bothered. The controversial Jimmy Connors actually came to the press box to make phone calls.

Bud Collins of *The Boston Globe* was the kingpin in North Conway. Bud welcomed everyone. One day he warmed up Laver in the morning and ran a press tournament for reporters in late afternoon after the matches were over. (Bud was a very good player. He won a national indoor mixed doubles tournament in 1959.)

Tournament director Jim Westhall had been a genius in bringing the world's top men to this tiny resort town. Westhall was a very capable organizer, and he was ambitious. He eventually moved the tournament to Vermont and finally, to New Haven, Conn. He was always seeking larger venues, more fans, and greater visibility. There was talk he would be named director of the U.S. Open in New York, but he didn't have the tennis creds. He was "only" a marketing man with roots in New Jersey.

These self-directed assignments were great. A half-hour interview with Ilie Nastase, No. 2 in the world? A sit-down with Ken Rosewall, one of the legends of the game.

On another occasion, I played Bobby Riggs in Portland as a promotion for the Volvo tournament. It was just three games. This was after the memorable match with Billie Jean King, and it drew several hundred fans. He let me win, 2-1.

Because filing from afar was appealing to me, I managed to obtain press credentials to the Super Bowl in 1976. It was in Miami and featured the Pittsburgh Steelers with quarterback Terry Bradshaw and the Dallas Cowboys with Roger Staubach.

Veteran journalists from Boston who were covering the event included Will McDonough, Leigh Montville, and Ray Fitzgerald of *The Boston Globe*, as well as TV's Clark Booth and radio's Gil Santos.

The nicest guy in Miami was Jim Snyder, aka Jimmy the Greek, a betting specialist for CBS. A group of Boston journalists went to his suite, where he was hosting an open house. He was very gracious. When he found this young outsider from Portland, he personally got me a drink and led me to the buffet. The Greek didn't have to welcome a small fish, but he did. Years later, CBS fired him for offensive remarks about black athletes.

The Super Bowl is one of the most-hyped events in all sports. As such, it is a dream assignment for those who like to avoid winter in the tundra. There is a two-week run-up between the season's end and the Super Bowl. Hundreds of scribes flee the northern cities to spend two weeks in the warm-weather clime that hosts the championship. Today, the Big Game acts as a huge industry convention for those involved with football. It is bro meets bro, and many cards are exchanged.

The *Press Herald* paid for my room and ground expenses. The ticket (press pass) to the game was, of course, free.

Covering the Super Bowl provided an early appreciation of how much energy goes into promotion and marketing on the national level. Pro football itself is not very interesting. Actual playing time is only about fourteen minutes per game, when you subtract timeouts, walking back to the huddle, and ad-driven inventions such as the two-minute warning.

But the league and all teams put enormous time and energy into promotion. If newspapers had been able to promote themselves, they might not have disappeared so easily. But print media, unlike TV or professional sports, does not have the mindset to promote.

At the Super Bowl, players and coaches are required to meet with the media, even when they have nothing to say. PR staffers hand out statistics, quotes and analysis after each quarter, so a sportswriter could be in Botswana and still file a credible story.

Pete Rozelle, NFL commissioner in 1976, was among the most adroit sports executives in modern sports history when it came to dealing with the media. He had come out of public relations in Los Angeles and had an answer for every question. He came to the media hospitality room almost every evening and answered questions for at least an hour.

Vicki was gracious in letting me wing off to Florida for the Super Bowl. The temperature fell to minus 25 in Kennebunk while I was gone. It was even cold in Miami. It hit 55 degrees the night before the game. Pittsburgh beat Dallas, 21-17. It was remembered as one of the best Super Bowls for many years.

Regarding life in Kennebunk, Vicki was generous in agreeing to take in Gia, my grandmother. In about 1978, Gia lost her sight. It had been coming on for several years following an episode of glaucoma. Now she was at the stage of having no sight at all.

Gia had been wonderful to our family over the years. She had purchased a summer home on Canandaigua Lake (N.Y.) for Dale and me to enjoy. As a buyer of suits and coats at Sibley, Lindsay and Curr in Rochester, she provided us with fine wardrobes as well as summer vacations. She was a key factor in paying our tuitions: me at Franklin and Marshall and Dale at Gettysburg College. When she went blind, she was invited to Maine.

Vicki was the key factor. Her family had taken in her grandfather when he needed help, so she was comfortable in agreeing to host a new resident. But first, she moved into a very large residence in Kennebunkport that was taking in older women. It was the Captain Lord Mansion, a gorgeous period home that is still operating. Gia had her own room and bathroom. She came downstairs for lunch and dinner. Her friends at the mansion were other women her age. Though Gia could not see, she developed a social life there.

On weekends she would have dinner with us. She loved being with Leslie and Drew, who would help her find the food on her plate. Both tiny children were loving.

On one Sunday afternoon, I took the children and Gia out to lunch at a nearby restaurant. Vicki stayed home. On this very memorable occasion, Leslie, Drew, Gia, and I were seated, and a waitress brought rolls and butter. Gia started telling a story.

Leslie had to go to the bathroom. Without interrupting Gia, I quietly took the three-year-old Leslie to the men's room, as she hadn't quite mastered her elimination skills.

She was placed in a stall. My blind grandmother was still talking, unaware that we had left. Tiny Drew had reached across the table and grabbed the basket of rolls. He began throwing them around the room.

When I returned, it took me a few moments to retrieve the rolls on the floor and appease the other diners. A cranky old fellow leaving the men's room growled, "There is a little girl in there wandering around. Is she yours?"

Leslie was collected, washed, and returned to the table. Gia was still talking. Drew was eating a roll but had spilled his water. We finished the meal and returned home without incident. Drew later used this anecdote in his writing exercises in elementary school. Vicki enjoyed the story, in part because she had avoided the crisis.

Vicki was very generous. First, she supported me in my globetrotting career. (You will hear of many more long-distance adventures.) And at this point in the late '70s, she was much in favor of "taking on" Gia. In a couple years, my grandmother would move into our house.

In 2025, Vicki needs a great deal of support because she had numerous orthopedic issues. In the past couple years, she has had two hip replacements (one had to be redone) and two shoulder replacements. In this same period, she broke her leg, her wrist, and her shoulder. In the future, she will have surgery on her right wrist.

She needs a lot of help. She gets it from me. Happily.

Life at the *Press Herald* was good. In subsequent years when my career was stalled, I look back on the '70s with fondness. My new projects at the newspaper worked.

I was always trying something new. I left the sports department to become the entertainment editor. In the first year of writing about bands, music, and local theater, I gained management approval to launch a weekly music supplement known as "Soundtrack" in the *Maine Sunday Telegram.*

This developed because in 1978, the Cumberland County Civic Center was built in downtown Portland. It held about 8,000. When the center opened with the sold-out appearance of rockers ZZ Top, it became apparent that money could be made from this form of entertainment.

Maine had had major acts in the past. The big bands, Frank Sinatra, and Ella Fitzgerald were among the major artists who had played at the Old Orchard Beach pier and other summer venues.

But the Civic Center was open all year. Promoters and band managers were happy to add Portland to a New England tour that might include Hartford, Worcester, and Boston. Those who entertained in the early years included rockers Bob Seger, Queen, Heart, Cheap Trick, and the Grateful Dead. Country stars like Kenny Rogers, Emmy Lou Harris, and Charlie Daniels appeared, as did jazz luminaries Al Hirt, Chuck Mangione, and Kenny G. Legends like Joan Baez and Bob Dylan also checked in, though not on the same bill.

The supplement was a money-maker for the company because it brought in revenue from advertisers targeting nightclubs, restaurants, recording companies and apparel stores. This was a new source of revenue. "Soundtrack" and my weekly entertainment column targeted a "younger demographic," as the advertising crowd would say. Newspapers appealed mostly to the older set, and "Soundtrack" reversed that trend. The civic center was one of the early examples of Portland becoming a happening city.

Music wasn't my sweet spot, but curiosity was a strength. I absorbed information and translated it into readable copy.

During this period of covering nightlife, I produced a concert of my own. I rented a venue, signed up three local bands and then publicized the event. It drew a crowd of several hundred who paid $4 per ticket. Sponsors included Budweiser beer and a local record company.

An embarrassing moment almost ruined my show. It started with a female singer. She was having boy trouble and left the "green room" in a hurry. I caught up with her outside and convinced her that the show must go on. The problem was, I couldn't get back into the club. A muscular 6-foot 10-inch security guard was covering the door. But I hadn't met him.

He wouldn't admit me when I returned to announce the next act. When I argued, he threatened to toss me on the street. One of the performers finally recognized the "promoter" and prevailed upon the conscientious bouncer to let me return.

Organizing an event like this was unprofessional. It could never be done at the *Globe*. The notion of an entertainment editor promoting music events smacks of a conflict of interest. *Press Herald* editor John K. Murphy warned me not to do it again.

Another unusual project was my trip to Lake Placid for the 1980 Winter Olympics. A big local band, The Blend, was playing for a week in the small community in New York state. I envisioned a big feature story about "life on the road," and I traveled with the band and equipment to the snow-bound town.

We arrived in Lake Placid to learn that our rooms were apartment units in the same building as the club. This was great. Lake Placid does not have many hotel rooms. Indeed, some ticket holders had to stay 50 miles from the town because there were no rooms. But I was in the middle of town. For free.

I watched the competition by day and hung around the club by night, when The Blend played for about four hours. Much-revered Eric Heiden won gold medals in skating; the U.S. hockey team beat the Soviet Union. That was lionized by ABC-TV, and telecaster Jim McKay called it the "miracle on ice," in part because the U.S. players were collegians. The Russians were state-compensated professional players.

In about a week, a pretty good feature story appeared about The Blend.

10

My First Book

In the late '70s, the blockbuster TV series *Roots* captivated the nation. Many Americans were suddenly interested in their ethnic backgrounds.

Maine had few Black residents. Our minority was the Franco-Americans, who had come south from Quebec to work in the mills of Lewiston, Auburn, Waterville, Winslow, Biddeford, Saco, Brunswick, and many other communities. This large migration took place from about 1870 to 1920. If there was a fast-moving river in Maine, there was likely to be a textile mill or a shoe factory on its banks. By the late 1970s, close to 40 percent of Maine residents had some French blood. Many older Mainers still spoke French on the street.

My mentor, Bob Moorehead, had moved from being sports editor to serving as the editor of the *Maine Sunday Telegram*. Bob approved the idea of giving me six weeks to travel around Maine in a company car for interviews with Franco-Americans. The goal was to write a multi-part series in the *Telegram*, which circulated throughout the whole state.

The story of Maine's Franco-Americans had not been told. Every French resident, from loom cleaner to shift manager, was interested in talking to me.

The title was "Quiet Presence: Stories of Franco-Americans in New England." Most of the book was about Maine families, but mill cities like Lowell and Lawrence, Mass., and Manchester, N.H., were also included so the book would have wider geographic appeal.

Regarding their migration, the French actually had a convenient situation compared to immigrants from distant lands such as the Irish, the Greeks and European Jews. The French could go "home" when they chose. Many young Francos worked in the mills of New England during the winter and returned to family farms in summer. I did research on one century-old photo that showed a dozen young (eighteen to twenty-five) mill hands in Sanford, Maine, in about 1912. All of them went back to Quebec in the summer.

European immigrants could not easily do that. Those who came from across the sea could rarely go back. They might have jobs but rarely saved enough money to return, even for a visit.

Though many historians have concluded that the mills exploited the workers, my research did not reflect that. True, by 1912 or so, most mills were dirty and paid low wages. A famous study by federal photographer Lewis Hine showed images of dank workplaces and dirty, butt-smoking youngsters.

But "history" is influenced by those who write it.

Many of the original immigrants were glad to have the jobs. Those fleeing persecution in Russia or famine in Ireland were saved by employment in the mills of New England.

One woman in Westbrook remembered (in 1979) being taken to a textile mill with her mother each day. The mill had a form of day care. Mom would work while kids played in another area. At lunchtime, mom and kids could eat together. This woman, Emma Tourangeau, was in her eighties when we talked, so she was referencing the turn of the century. A smiling extrovert, she expressed great satisfaction with her life. Her photo appeared on the back cover of the book.

This series was an enormous success, in part because no one had taken the time to chronicle the French-Canadians. When the Gannett Publishing Co., which owned the Press Herald, launched a book division, I wrote a full-length tome. (Note: The Gannett Publishing Co. was a separate entity from the Gannett Group that owns *USA Today* and many other enterprises.)

The term "Quiet Presence" was chosen because the Franco-Americans were not vocal in their communities. They were not politically active nor were they complainers. They were slow to assimilate, perhaps because they still had ties to their family homes in Quebec. Many Franco-Americans still spoke French. Some "Anglo" schools forbid French in the playgrounds because they felt those who kept their French did not become fluent in English.

Quiet Presence sold close to 10,000 copies, which is a significant total for a regional history. The *Maine Sunday Telegram* would run a (free) quarter-page advertisement each Sunday, which helped sales. Some schools bought the book in bulk to be used in classrooms.

Because this was the first such narrative, clubs and organizations in Maine invited me to speak. There were about thirty slides, and I presented a rather heroic story that many had never heard. The Biddeford-Saco Rotary gave me a standing ovation after I spoke. It brought me to tears. Acclaim must be what drives journalists.

My favorite research trip in writing the book was to the St. John Valley, in northernmost Maine. These Francos were called Acadians, because they had originally come from Acadia, or the Atlantic maritime provinces. They were potato farmers who still spoke French. Including farmers with mill workers gave the book a more inclusive feel.

Of the seven books I have written by 2025, most contained numerous interviews with "people on the ground." Many professional historians (defined here as professors with advanced degrees) do not interview the "great unwashed." The work with statistics and data. My interviews give my books a different sound and feel.

Looking back, so much was happening in 1980!

We had healthy tots aged four and two. My blind grandmother lived with us, and she was thankful to do so. We employed a wonderful full-time babysitter, Susan Wilson. Vicki was a very popular sales executive with WGAN-TV. We moved to Portland to be close to our jobs. We owned a fine five-bedroom house adjacent to the University of Southern Maine. We also owned a five-unit apartment building in South Portland.

And then a life-changing event occurred. We moved. Again.

Above left: Audrey Hepburn, a beloved actress whose press conferences in Hollywood drew capacity crowds.

Above right: The dignified Arthur Ashe, a great player and a succinct interviewee.

Above left: Pioneering environmentalist Rachel Carson visited Plum Island, Newburyport, in 1947.

Above right: Garrulous tennis journalist Bud Collins, with the author.

Veteran performer Ted Danson sometimes asked questions of interviewers.

The energetic Doris Kearns Goodwin offers anecdotes that make history come alive.

Above left: Robert Duvall was perfect for his role in *Lonesome Dove*.

Above right: Author Elmore Leonard created off-beat characters that made his novels novel.

The Boston Globe has been a force in journalism for decades.

Left: Journalists visited Bob Hope's house in Hollywood on frequent occasions. He was a non-stop promoter.

Below: The Eagle is a majestic hallmark of the Coast Guard.

Ken Burns became a national figure for his productions for PBS.

Billie Jean King and Bobby Riggs tested each on the court in 1973. I hit with Riggs when he was in Portland, and he said I had a good American twist serve.

Above left: Historian Jill Lepore appeared at the Newburyport Literary Festival.

Above right: Michael Lewis is among my favorite historians.

George Mitchell was a soft-spoken but effective senator from Maine, and a friend of our family.

Right: A small wooden vessel at repose on the Merrimack River, Newburyport.

Below: The Hendrickson family, plus Sen. George Mitchell: Leslie, Mitchell, Vicki, Dyke, and Drew.

Left: Robert Mitchum would submit to interviews, but his answers were terse in the extreme.

Below: I spent a day on the road with Sen. Edmund Muskie when I was with the *Press Herald* in Portland. He campaigned in filthy mills and dreary shoe factories, and later proposed measures for cleaner working conditions.

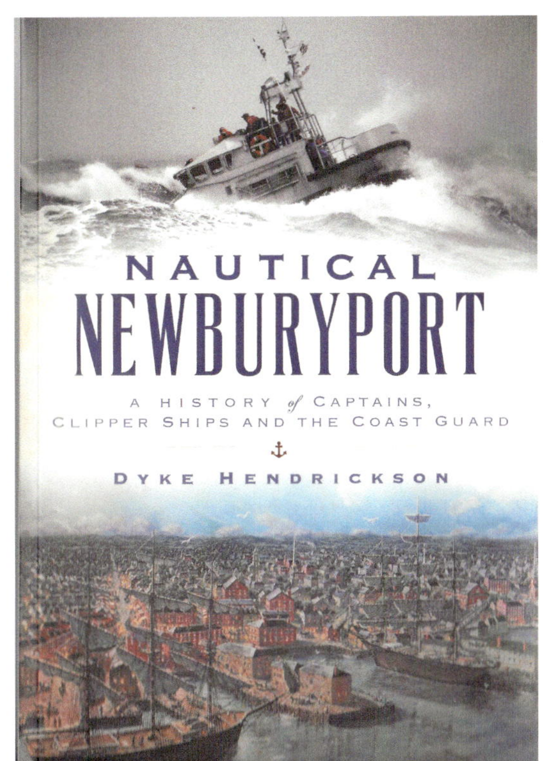

Right: Here is the cover of my book about the local waterfront, titled *Nautical Newburyport*.

Below: Newburyport, Mass., is the birthplace of the Coast Guard (1790).

Petaluma, Calif., is the city where I got my first newspaper job.

NBA coach Rick Pitino was a great coach but an uncooperative interviewee.

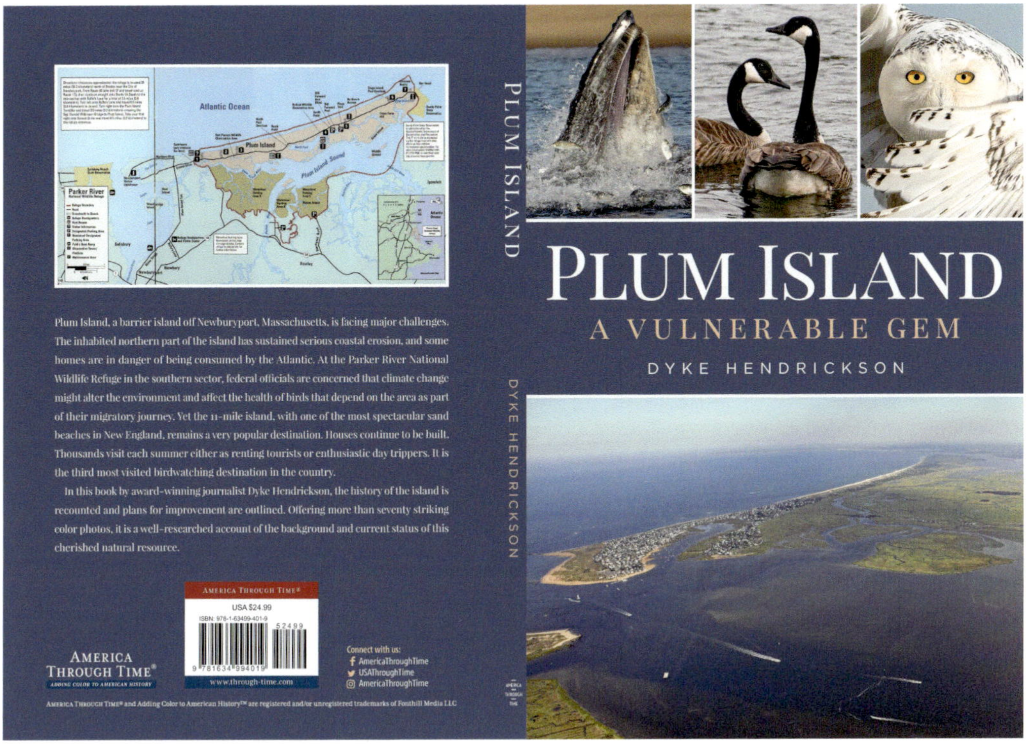

The cover of my book about Plum Island, a barrier island off Newburyport.

Above left: CBS anchor Dan Rather often appeared at the Hollywood Press Tour, which I covered for the *Boston Herald*.

Above right: ABC-TV executive Roone Arledge was a pioneer in sports coverage. I interviewed him in the Rainbow Room in New York.

Author Richard Russo, once an instructor at Colby College, became a national figure with the publication of *Nobody's Fool.*

Barbara Walters was a durable asset at ABC-TV. She reminded me that she was from the Boston area when I interviewed her in New York.

The *Yankee Clipper* is a tourist vessel that operates out of Newburyport. Thousands cruise up the Merrimack River each summer.

Fishing boats are few in Newburyport these days—but pleasure boats and visiting yachts are often seen on the waterfront.

Left: The *Boston Herald* was owned by magnate Rupert Murdoch when I was the TV columnist there in the '80s.

Below: A few lobster boats still work out of Newburyport. The lobster is one denizen of the North Atlantic that is still healthy and marketable.

Sen. Ted Kennedy generated electricity among audiences, especially in mill towns like Sanford, Maine, where I covered his campaign stop on behalf of Sen. Ed Muskie.

Author Anita Shreve, who appeared at the Newburyport Literary Festival, was taken too early at age seventy-one.

Above: Actress Tea Leoni (*The Ambassador*) wanted some publicity in the Boston market, so her agent set up a one-on-one lunch with me at Pier 4 restaurant.

Left: Dan Healey is a lobsterman and benefactor in Newburyport.

11

We Relocate to Mississippi, Work in New Orleans

In 1981, we moved from Portland to the Gulf community of Pass Christian, Mississippi. The culprit was ambition. And giddy optimism.

Perhaps because I grew up near New York, my goal was to work on a big-city newspaper. My father brought home numerous newspapers which I closely read, including the *Herald-Tribune*, the *Journal-American*, and *The New York Times*. Succeeding in Portland did not seem like it should be the apex of my career.

My goal was *The Boston Globe*. I had a serious interview with *The Boston Globe*, considered the premiere newspaper in New England. It was set up by Will McDonough, the late *Globe* sportswriter. We played tennis together at the Patriots summer training camp. There were several candidates for one job. The sports editor, Dave Smith, did not hire me.

Joining the *Globe* did not mean all would be good. They already had Bud Collins covering tennis. McDonough and others were writing about the NFL. It wasn't a given that I would thrive. Indeed, some writers who joined the prestigious *Globe* spent their years in "velvet handcuffs." They had the cache of working for the top newspaper in New England and they were well paid. But they couldn't advance.

The failure to get the job at the *Globe* made me look in other directions.

Vicki had grown up in Memphis. She went to Mississippi State College for Women. I had hitchhiked to New Orleans during my senior year in college. In 1980, when she returned from a trip to the South one spring, I blurted out, "Let's move. How about near New Orleans?"

Vicki had just visited her college roommate, Patti Ryan. Patti had co-written the song, "Looking for Love in All the Wrong Places," a huge hit which has become part of the American lexicon. Patti lived in Biloxi, Miss. They had great fun together. Why not move to the Mississippi Coast, near New Orleans?

Vicki secured a job at the CBS-TV affiliate WLOX in Biloxi, so we had one job. That company paid moving expenses.

We were thirty-five. We were energetic. We often talked about "investing in memories." We went south.

It was an enormous undertaking. We had two young children and a blind grandmother. We had a comfortable five-bedroom house that was stuffed with furniture a college friend had given us after she inherited a farmhouse in Connecticut. But we did it.

When I gave notice at the newspaper, no one could believe it. The editors and reporters were shocked. Everything was going so well.

Many readers appreciated my coverage. No one had ever covered tennis, skiing, nightlife, or the Franco-Americans. People liked me. They loved Vicki.

Friends and colleagues did not know what to say, especially since I did not have a job at the other end.

What a risk! And what trouble developed. The strains were enormous. We almost got divorced.

The trip down was fine and we moved into a handsome condominium development in scenic Ocean Springs, Miss., while we looked for a house. Most of our furniture was stored.

Vicki went to work. I minded the kids and Gia. Soon I got a job as a bartender at an oyster bar to keep me in walking-around money. I sought jobs at a newspaper in Mobile, about 60 miles away and also in Jackson, Miss., about 200 miles away. That was very unrealistic. Could we really move to Jackson after coming all the way to the Gulf Coast? In this case, youth should not be wasted on the young.

I applied to the Biloxi newspaper also. But no job was offered.

The rejections led to great angst. The decision to leave a fine life in Portland looked ridiculous. A reason for leaving the "grind" of the job in Portland was to have more time off. Now there was too much empty time.

But we kept going. We looked for houses to buy; we went out to dinner at fine seafood restaurants. We listened to Patti Ryan play "Looking for Love" in local roadhouses.

In July: a big break. *The Times-Picayune* in New Orleans hired me. It was on the copy desk, editing stores and writing headlines. This was not a dream job, but it was essential for money and peace of mind.

We bought a large, fully air-conditioned house in Pass Christian, Miss. That is 65 miles east of New Orleans and about 35 miles west of Biloxi, where Vicki worked. No sane couple would be happy with so much commuting with two toddlers and a blind octogenarian at home. But we were relieved to land somewhere.

The kids were put into a nearby preschool; Gia moved into her own room with a private bath. This was a terrific house. It had a glittering cement swimming pool in the back and a large cabana. Half of the cabana could be used as an air-conditioned office; the other half was a screened-in porch looking out at the pool.

The house itself had four bedrooms and two baths. Also included was a full apartment with a bathroom. The brick residence came with a fireplace and an outdoor deck. In winter after some leaves disappeared, one could see the shining Gulf of Mexico only 200 yards away. On the one-acre parcel was an enormous live oak tree that must have been around during the Civil War. Mature azalea and wisteria bushes bordered the property. Dogwoods abounded. Honeysuckle exuded sweet fragrances.

Much of my time was spent in New Orleans. Vicki had to organize the children and Gia. Many of Vicki's memories are of frustrating hours of supervising the household. Vicki did a wonderful job.

Gia, though blind, was flexible. She got to like her new home. She was a native of North Carolina, and she liked the weather. Once we found Edna, a very caring (paid) companion, Gia enjoyed going outside for walks. It was always warm. During the long Maine winters, even an Adm. Byrd would have trouble enjoying Portland. If Gia had fallen on the ever-present ice, the final years of her life could have been ruined.

Gia listened to books on tape. She read several per week, and we would discuss them. She liked talking with the children. The kids, the books and her walks in the warm Mississippi air kept her sane. She once said she liked the Pass Christian set-up better than that in Portland.

Vicki bore the heavy lifting of our awkward situation. One associated problem was that we could not get household help. In Portland, there had been many educated, middle-class young women who were pleased with a day job. In Mississippi, we could not find the right person.

Much tension developed. Vicki did not like her job. It was sales. Her customers ranged from a catfish restaurant to an alligator farm (for tourists). There was little intellectual stimulation. Many of the men she worked with were sexist rednecks. Vicki has enormous talent. She would go on to create the Newburyport Literary Festival. She earned a master's degree at the University of New Hampshire. And then she started the Newburyport Adult and Community Education Program. But in Mississippi, she had no outlet for her creativity and energy.

She prevailed until we could move again.

Meanwhile, the former hot-shot Dyke Hendrickson hated the copy desk. Transition to a writing job was not permitted. The supervisor of the copy desk would not approve a transfer. He felt newcomers would start as copy editors with the goal of quickly moving to the writing side. He was correct. So it was no dice for a reporter's job at *The Times-Picayune.*

The editor was Charles Ferguson. The copy desk editor, whom I learned to detest, was Tom Gregory. The news editor was Jim Amoss. Jim would rise to become the editor of *The Times-Picayune.* I met him (again) at our daughter's graduation from Columbia School of Journalism.

A promising young reporter at the time was Dean Baquet, who later became editor of *The New York Times.*

The Times-Picayune was almost wiped out by Hurricane Katrina in 2005. In recent years, it has been taken over by a publishing company in Baton Rouge. Almost all veterans at *The Times-Picayune* were fired (in 2018), so the new news organization could be restructured. It now comes out only a few times per week. The failure of a daily newspaper in New Orleans is another indication that the print profession is doomed.

Also in New Orleans, I tried to write a part-time tennis column. With 300,000 readers, *The Times-Picayune* circulation area had a lot of players, teams, and tournaments. I had a sheaf of clips from Wimbledon and Forest Hills. But the editors did not encourage slugs on the copy desk to be creative. Again, a request to do some freelance reporting was turned down. Book reviews were permitted. That was the only good thing that happened in my three years there. There was no payment, but the library now includes many tomes from the LSU Press.

Great frustration developed. Editing stories and writing headlines eight hours per day was not in my career plan.

I still ask, where did the idea come from that great things would happen to me? My cautious, taciturn father had not been an achiever. My mother was very bright but happy to stay in the suburbs. Post-children, she was a substitute teacher and a part-time movie reviewer for local (free) newspapers.

I had such high expectations after a successful decade in Portland. And nerve. I was willing to take risks. I don't know where that came from. But I hit the wall at *The Times-Picayune*.

Job aspirations aside, New Orleans was a colorful and exciting news city.

During my few years on the copy desk, we had a plane crash that killed 190. That is tragic but it was a huge story. The newsroom was abuzz for weeks, first as we covered the "breaking news" and later when the follow-up stories were developed. The reason for the crash: wind shear.

There was a lot of random crime in New Orleans, which is also news. Each day the newspaper ran a crime log of muggings, shootings and break-ins. This was a well-read feature of the newspaper. But these stories became unnerving. Many scary events were taking place in the neighborhood in which I stayed some nights.

My room was in an apartment in a neighborhood known as the Irish Channel. The unit was owned by a social worker from Chicago named John Mann. Nice guy. It was at the corner of Magazine and Washington Streets, adjacent to the Garden District. The police log was constantly noting crimes of violence in my neighborhood.

The log of victims almost included me. Once a group of local guys chased a mugger right to my door. "He's got a gun," someone called out. Our door was locked. But still, I hit the floor. The vigilantes eventually left. The miscreant must have gotten away.

Another time, a shooting almost took place while I was getting gas at a station on a Saturday morning. A speeding car hit the brakes like one would do in a movie. The driver got out of the car with a pistol in his hand. A film, I thought? But there was no crew. In fact, there were no station attendants. They had seen this nasty guy packing heat, and they fled in the opposite direction.

The gun-toting driver entered the station office and then left. Without shooting. I remained motionless in an aging, yellow Rabbit, thinking "Don't shoot me, I'm only the copy editor."

Crime was always on people's minds. In the three-year duration that I was in New Orleans, four members of our twenty-person copy desk were robbed at gunpoint. One was shot in the mid-section even after he had given up his wallet.

Largely because of crime, we did not consider moving to New Orleans. I did not want my name showing up in the crime log or the obituary section. Living on the coast made for a long commute, but it was safe. And there was a lot to do.

There was a lively tennis crowd, and matches took place every weekend. We could play at night, even in January, because it never got very cold. We joined the Pass Christian Yacht Club. We didn't have a boat but went for lunch every Sunday after church. Gia enjoyed getting out.

The restaurants in New Orleans were fabulous. Our favorite was Mr. Bs, in the French Quarter. We also liked Commander's Palace, near the apartment in the Garden District. When our marriage started getting shaky, Vicki would come into New Orleans every couple weeks, and we would enjoy a terrific meal together.

We took the kids to Mardi Gras and slept over in the apartment. We went to JazzFest. We visited with newspaper colleagues in the city. But for the first time, there were no media events or conferences. Copy editors don't qualify for media credentials. The easy access because of a press pass had come to an end.

In Pass Christian, having a pool in the backyard was heaven. The kids were taught to swim. Tennis lessons took place at a manicured park nearby. The park had historic guns that had been used in the Civil War—against Yankees.

But the driving was killing us. Pelting rainstorms that were so heavy that the road ahead could not be seen. Yet one could not pull off the road because truckers might be parked there. The rain was so fierce the trucks could not be seen! Several times my Rabbit broke down on the I-10.

Vicki was also driving a lot. Once she drove about 100 miles from a business appointment in Hattiesburg, Miss., to the French Quarter just to have dinner.

One project launched during the days in New Orleans was research on a book to be titled *The Right Bank*. During the 1920s, scores of young writers and artists came to New Orleans. The living was cheap. Prohibition was not strictly enforced. Luminaries who spent time in the French Quarter during the '20s included William Faulkner and his mentor, Sherwood Anderson.

Faulkner was just getting started. Anderson was a titan, though Faulkner ended up mocking the older man. Others included F. Scott Fitzgerald, John Dos Passos, Jean Toomer, Lyle Saxon, and Anita Loos.

Loos was probably the most successful published author there. She was a scriptwriter in Hollywood. And she wrote the blockbuster bestseller *Gentlemen Prefer Blondes*, which was made into a popular film. But she didn't linger long in New Orleans, perhaps because the ego-driven young men were so self-absorbed.

Local scribe Oliver LaFarge won the Pulitzer Prize in 1929 for *Native Son*.

There were dozens more who are not recalled today.

There had been a book titled *The Left Bank* that lionized those who were on the Left Bank of Paris, including Hemingway, Gertrude Stein, *et al.* My book was to be titled *The Right Bank*. I sent out numerous queries, but no publishers were interested.

Nothing much was working in 1983. We began going to marriage counseling.

Vicki and I have dissimilar personalities. She is a vociferous extrovert. I am an intense introvert. She is from the South; I am a native of the Northeast. She wanted a stable family life; I was chasing a glorious career. We were both risk-takers, which sometimes can have troublesome results.

Vicki was not reluctant to make her dissatisfaction known. Can you blame her? For my part, guilt for bringing us so far from home was ever present. Our marriage counselor expressed wonder that we were together in the first place. He suggested that we consider divorce.

In the summer of 1983, we returned to Portland for a vacation. We loved being back in Maine. It seemed like home. As we returned to the Gulf Coast after a lovely visit, it truly seemed like we were going in the wrong direction.

12

Return to New England

The source of the job openings in those days was a trade magazine known as *Editor and Publisher*. An entry calling for a TV editor at the *Boston Herald* appeared. My earnest application followed.

Media mogul Rupert Murdoch had recently bought the *Herald*. It was part of his early entry in the U.S. media market. To change the profile of the *Herald*, he essentially dismissed everyone on the editorial side. That meant lots of jobs were available.

The *Boston Herald* had a circulation (unaudited) of about 360,000. It put emphasis on sports, police news and TV coverage. This was because Murdoch was planning on acquiring TV stations in major markets. So why not fill the pages of his newspapers with stories and photos about television?

Murdoch's revitalization of the *Herald* proved to be one of the last strategic investments in an urban newspaper in the U.S. Newspapers started fading in the '90s, and soon the word was out on Wall Street that print media was done. *The New York Times*' purchase of *The Boston Globe* in 1993 for $1.1 billion is viewed as one of the greatest financial mistakes in publishing history.

In recent years, billionaire *Globe* owner John Henry has moved the newspaper out of the building on Morrissey Boulevard and into an office building with printing in a suburban plant. The *Boston Herald*, too, has sold its property in downtown Boston. On that topic, the *Portland Press Herald* moved out of its long-time headquarters on Congress Street. The building at 390 Congress St. was converted into a hotel named The Press.

But in the mid-'80s, the *Herald* was a dynamic property that Murdoch doted on so he could get into the television market.

Editors at the *Herald* liked my application. They flew me to the Hub for a three-day tryout. This visit was nerve-wracking because this job was really important. It seemed to be our chance to get back to New England, where we still had many friends.

During my tryout, they had me editing stories and writing a few short stories. Editor Joe Robinowitz and other editors mostly wanted to meet me to determine whether I would fit.

Working for a tabloid was new. There was a high percentage of crime and mayhem stories. New Orleans had more mayhem than Boston. But the *Herald* seemed to treat them like entertainment. "Three Dead in South Boston Fire; Mom Said Good-Bye as She Fell Through Collapsing Floor."'

Actually, the *Herald-American*, which preceded the *Herald*, had published one of the most famous fire photos in newspaper history. Photographer Stanley Foreman was on the ground when a woman jumped from a burning building. He caught her in mid-air, with a look of panic and horror. She died. But his photo has lived and has won many awards.

After a few weeks, Robinowitz called with a job offer. Ebullience ensued. Vicki was pleased, too, but it meant she would be packing and moving the kids once again.

My annual salary at the *Herald* was a paltry $30,000 with no overtime. "We don't negotiate," warned editor Robinowitz, who was making six figures and living in the high-end suburb of Weston.

That was a very low salary, even for 1984. Perhaps this demonstrates a fatal flaw in the minds of liberal arts majors. The money was very bad, but the job sounded very interesting. My mission: create a TV section within the newspaper, produce the Sunday entertainment supplement, interview TV stars, and report on developments within the vibrant TV industry.

Though it meant more work, Vicki enjoyed the interregnum. She resigned from the TV station and got rid of our lousy help. She now had time to swim in the pool at night, attend the fascinating World's Fair in New Orleans, and hang out with her pal singer-songwriter Patti Ryan. She loved the opportunity to spend more time with our children.

Another reason that she appreciated her new situation: Her husband was not present.

In late December 1983, our little family traveled to Memphis for the holidays. From there, I drove to Boston. Vicki and the kids returned to coastal Mississippi to get ready to move. Another chapter for the traveling Hendricksons was beginning.

13

The Traveler's Tale: Boston

The transition to the Boston area was not smooth. We had not sold our house in Mississippi, so we were forced to rent for a year until we got organized. A decent three-bedroom house was found in suburban Lexington, about 20 miles from the *Herald.* But renting a house meant that we would have to move again when we finally bought a house.

We did "place" Gia with my sister, Dale, in Ann Arbor, Michigan. Gia was failing. But she didn't resent it. She told me several times during our walks in clement Pass Christian that she was "ready to go." Gia was not ill. She was just losing her life.

The fact that she had not gone bonkers living alone in a single room upstairs reflected great strength. She had been a very successful business executive, full of energy and a recipient of accolades. Before she lost her sight, she had been re-recruited by Associated Dry Goods to run clothing departments at its new branches outside of Rochester.

Though totally blind, she was able to cope when she was moved to Kennebunkport, Portland, Ocean Springs, Pass Christian, and finally to an extended care facility in Ann Arbor. She died there peacefully at eighty-six.

Perhaps her strength came from a life of defeating adversity. A native of Winston-Salem, N.C., she had come to New York in 1920. She was a single mother after a brief marriage. She knew no one in the largest city in the U.S. She got a job as a "shop girl," selling coats and suits. Later she worked at the Tailored Woman, a leading fashion retailer. My mother, Eloise, initially had babysitters. In high school, she was ordered to come straight home and do her homework.

Edith and Eloise prevailed. My very bright mother skipped a grade, was an honor roll student and graduated from Hood College, in Frederick, Maryland, in 1940.

The *Herald* had agreed to pay moving costs. It must have been $20,000 even then. We had eight rooms of furniture and a grand piano. Editor Joe Robinowitz angrily waved the moving bill in my face, but the company paid it.

The job started on January 8, 1984. For the first two weeks, the company put me in the Sheraton Hotel in the downtown. During this fortnight I visited the real estate office of Boston University. They had a very small studio at 850 Beacon St. It was furnished, and it became mine for a monthly rent of $200. Let the TV games begin.

Working at the *Herald* was exciting. Many PR operatives coveted my attention.

The *Herald* was very much the No. 2 newspaper in town. All PR people started their publicity initiatives by pitching the *Globe*. But Boston was the fifth largest TV market in the country. PR reps sought out the *Herald* if they struck out at the *Globe*. At the *Times-Picayune*, I had been a lowly copy editor, a frustrated nobody. At the *Herald*, I was suddenly a happening guy.

Soon, an "average day" might call for having lunch with Tea Leone in Hollywood or interviewing Pierce Brosnan at dinner in New York.

The *Herald* was a low-end tabloid. A story it followed closely during my first couple of years was "The Professor and the Prostitute." A professor at Tufts Medical School had fallen in love with a prostitute. She was attractive, evidently fun, and friendly. She had ties with numerous members of the New England Patriots football team.

The prostitute went missing. It turned out the professor had murdered her in a moment of jealousy and had buried her body in a landfill outside of the city. It seemed like the *Herald* assigned staffers every time a backhoe was sent to a recycling center.

The professor went to the slammer. He was released after about a dozen years. Understandably, he did not want to give an exit interview to the *Herald*.

We ran many unflattering stories about Sen. Ted Kennedy. Freelance photographers would take boats into Hyannis Harbor, waiting for Kennedy to go sailing. If they caught the portly Ted looking bad in a bathing suit, that photo would make page 1. There was no story, just Ted being overweight.

The *Herald* said it had a circulation of 360,000. My goal had been to work in a big market and that had been achieved. But there is no inherent advantage. You don't get paid more based on circulation. And unlike TV reporters, the print provider rarely gets recognized. Possible explanation: Dreamers like me felt it might lead to better opportunities.

The family moved in the summer of 1984. We had rented in Lexington for a year but hated it. And we couldn't afford to buy there. As we were looking for houses in other towns, we saw a story in *Boston* magazine that listed communities described as "The Last Places to Buy a Mansion for $150,000."

One community listed was Newburyport, about 40 miles north of Boston. When we got there, there were no mansions for $150,000. That was a misleading headline and story. But we liked the community. Its population was 17,000. It was on the ocean and also on the Merrimack River. It had impressive nineteenth-century mansions on High Street that made the thoroughfare one of the most impressive in Massachusetts.

We drove out to Plum Island (a barrier island 5 miles east of the city). After seeing the majestic Atlantic, we went to The Grog—the hangout for locals—for a few beers. At the end of a fun day in a charming small city, we decided to buy in Newburyport.

This meant the kids had to start over in a new community and a new school. That is an ongoing regret: The kids had to start over so often.

That said, many families have faced significant change. Newcomers to this country adjusted and have achieved much. My rationalization was that our kids did not have it so bad. At the least, they didn't have to take transatlantic ships packed with people who didn't speak the language.

The position at the *Herald* enabled me to take the kids on interesting outings. Leslie, twelve, and Drew, ten, attended many events. Leslie still remembers the Whitney Houston concert on the Boston Common. Whitney was about twenty-two, beautiful, and energetic. We had terrific (free) seats, twentieth row, on the aisle. It was a very memorable performance.

Drew attended many Patriots and Red Sox games. Sometimes Leslie came, but she wasn't a sports fan. Vicki never wanted to attend, but she enjoyed the museums of Boston.

In the late '80s, each of the kids went to Hollywood for at least two weeks. The networks jointly hosted a "press tour," to which they invited TV writers and TV reporters to preview the new shows for the upcoming fall. NBC will have had three days of screening and interviews, and then CBS will have had three days, etc. Because the tour involved the major networks, PBS and various cable operations, the stay in first-class Hollywood hotels was two to three weeks.

They went separately and stayed in my room. Leslie met teen heart-throb Kirk Cameron. Drew had his picture taken with Vanna White.

One year Drew and I were being taken by limo to a media dinner at Bob Hope's house near Studio City. The limo offered a TV, drinks, and snack food. It was a big event, with many NBC stars and a real red carpet. I got out of the limo and was walking toward the entrance of Hope's place when it became clear that Drew was not with me. I hustled back to the limo. "Drew, please get out of the car. It's time to go the dinner." He asked, hopefully, "Can't I stay here watching the Dodgers' game until it's over?" "No, Drew, you will cause limo-lock. There are dozens of cars behind us."

At the large poolside gathering, Drew ended up sitting on the lap of Bob Hope. The entertainer was showing him his new watch, which reported the time from several international cities. Hope was a very accommodating guy and a nonstop promoter.

One of our biggest family (free) trips was to Disney World in Florida. The Disney company is energetic when it comes to promoting events to the media. On its fifteenth birthday, it invited hundreds of entertainment editors to Orlando. Everything was gratis: free plane tickets, free motel, free food.

Disney closed the park one evening, and the media and their families attended—for free. But it didn't make a good tale for the kids. When twelve-year-old Leslie told her friends that she didn't have to wait in lines and that the popcorn was free, none of her young friends believed her.

The *Herald* had no policy against taking freebies. Editors didn't seem to mind free tickets and week-long junkets. Regarding this trip to Disney World, four editors from the *Herald* attended. We actually hired a freelancer to write the story. (The Boston-based freelancer also attended for free.)

The *Herald* wanted stories, because Ruport Murdoch was promoting television and entertainment. The more TV stories that were produced, the happier his team of aggressive franchise builders would be. And indeed, the first local TV station he bought was in Boston. It was the beginning of the Fox network.

The TV beat was exceedingly interesting. One of the most riveting media productions was the making of *War and Remembrance* in 1989. This was the second part of Herman Wouk's saga about World War II, seen through the eyes of a waspish navy family and a Jewish clan with roots in Europe and America.

The cost for the lengthy miniseries was $100 million, which made it the most expensive TV production ever at the time. The attention to detail and drama was remarkable. Producers reconstructed the Auschwitz death camp to scale so final episodes would appear authentic. They were so good they were hard to watch.

The TV critics saw all episodes in advance and could interview stars such as Robert Mitchum, Jane Seymour, Robert Morley, and Polly Bergen. Journalists were invited to the wrap party on *Queen Mary II*. Thousands attended this party. Mitchum was seated at the first table to emphasize the star quality of the event. But few journalists glad-handed the gruff, venerable star.

The "talent" at my table was an actor who had played an officer on a German submarine. He was far from a star. Indeed, he seemed pleased that he had been invited to the mammoth gathering.

I did a seven-minute stand-up essay for one Boston television station recommending the series.

Another interesting presentation for the press corps was exposed to was *Lonesome Dove*, based on the book by Larry McMurtry. It had a colorful cast that included Robert Duvall, Tommy Lee Jones, Diane Lane, Jessica Huston, Danny Glover, and Robert Urich.

A press party was thrown at the Museum of the West in Los Angeles. The entire cast was there, enjoying Texas barbecue and Lone Star beer. At these events, it is acceptable for media folk to sit down next to a star, even if the star is with other people. The actors expect it.

Danny Glover and the affable Urich were at a table. I headed toward them for an interview. But someone stepped in my way. It was Gene Autry, the aging cowboy. When he saw my press badge that identified me as being from New England, he launched a long-winded recollection about his early days on a rodeo tour that had stretched from Worcester to Bangor. After Autry departed, Glover and Urich were gone. No interviews there.

In another event promoting *Lonesome Dove* that week, a descending elevator at the Universal Hotel in L.A. was taking me to a press conference. The lift stopped and picked up one passenger: actor Robert Duvall.

When he noted my press tour credential, he asked if I had previewed the show. "Yes." And then he inquired, earnestly, "How was my performance?"

There you go. Robert Duvall asking Dyke Hendrickson for affirmation. "Great. Very understated." He smiled and appeared pleased.

Most interviews with stars in Hollywood were pretty breezy, but sometimes executives got grilled. An awkward moment came at a session when an ABC program chief was asked why he passed on *The Cosby Show*. It might have been one of the biggest errors of judgment in modern TV history. He stammered that "the early scripts were not polished."

This Cosby series changed TV entertainment in the '80s. Because so many viewers watched Cosby, the series spawned hits of the shows that followed on the same evening, including *Cheers* and *Family Ties*. The success of a black cast paved the way for series such *In Living Color* and *The Fresh Prince of Bel Air*. It was said that Cosby saved NBC and the family series.

Bill Cosby was a hero on many fronts in the late '80s. He was lauded for championing thoughtful scripts that showcased successful middle-class black families. And Cosby offered roles to people of color. It is regrettable that Cosby was guilty of numerous offenses against women. It reminds me of a jailhouse slogan offered by convicts: "Please don't judge my whole life by my worst days."

Years later, O. J. Simpson was found not guilty of two murders and was released. But every situation is different.

TV reporters often mixed with stars. A network hosted a crowded cocktail party for the cast of *Dynasty*.

Dynasty was an enormous hit series in the '80s. Its producers gathered its world-renowned stars at a press event at a Hollywood hotel. I had just gotten a drink and a plate when Linda Evans appeared. The gorgeous blonde co-star asked if there were questions. Several innocuous questions were asked. Out of queries, I backed away. But then I walked into Joan Collins, the sexy brunette star. I almost dropped my meatballs.

A star who dazzled just about everybody on our press tour was Audrey Hepburn. She was in the final years of her memorable career and was starring in a lighthearted mystery with Robert Wagner titled *Love Among Thieves*, 1987. It was one of her last projects, and Hollywood knew that. She drew an enormous crowd to her press conference.

The media room at the Century Plaza Hotel was packed. Directors and producers from other studios and networks came; busboys, bellhops, and hotel beauticians snuck in to watch from the crowded perimeter. Audrey Hepburn was a star revered for her talent and for her humanitarian work.

A woman journalist asked, "Miss Hepburn, I know this sounds unprofessional, but how did you stay so thin for all these years."

Audrey nodded and smiled, as if she had heard the question before. "It wasn't a diet or self-control. I grew up in Europe during World War II. My family was dodging Nazis in Holland and Belgium. Because we were on the move, there often wasn't enough to eat. Later a doctor told me that my stomach had never developed because I was often without food. As a result, I could never eat very much. So, I didn't gain weight."

The vast audience, most of whom had heard everything in Hollywood, was mesmerized by the poignant tale. And the working journalists were pleased they had a new story line with which to introduce the venerable star.

Stars cooperated with the media. Most of the reporters had been "vetted," meaning PR reps from the network knew who they were inviting. They believed that the journalists would write reasonable stories for legitimate media. For instance, a reporter for the *Star* or *Enquirer* would not be invited.

Scribes on the press tour went to interesting places and met beautiful people in abetting the Hollywood publicity machine. We went to Larry Hagman's oceanside house in Malibu. There we watched Hagman, Linda Gray, and Victoria Principal chat amiably while a Tex-Mex band played "La Bamba" on the roof of a neighbor's garage. We went to the California Yacht Club, where the voluble Dolly Parton hopped from table to table promoting a new series. At the L.A. Zoo, Tom Wopat's country band played as part of a publicity event to draw attention to a coming TV production about urban zoos. The band had to stop playing because the loud music sent the chimps into a frenzy.

One of the favorites on the press tour was news magnate Ted Turner. The talkative mogul called many reporters by name. Sometimes he would comment on their stories. His willingness to cultivate individuals in the media was part of the reason he generated so much coverage for TBS.

Network anchors like Dan Rather, Peter Jennings, and Ted Koppel would appear to promote their shows and pontificate on the news. One of Rather's remarks when replying to criticism of CBS was, "The dogs bark but the caravan moves on." He seemed to be saying that he ignored most criticism.

One of my longest one-on-one interviews was with actress Tea Leoni. She was chosen as one of the stars for a remake of *Charlie's Angels*. The show was not aired. But she became a star in movies, and, later, with the TV series *Madame Secretary*.

Her "story" (put out by a PR team) was that she was casually surfing when her agent appeared on shore and waved a fax. The message indicated she had been picked for a Hollywood pilot. Tea caught a few more waves before returning to shore to hear the details, her bio indicated.

Another memorable aspect of my interview with Tea was that when glamorous actress Victoria Principal entered the restaurant, heads turned. Forks dropped. The sight of the *Dallas* star brought the room to momentary silence. It demonstrated that glamorous leading stars were still capable of generating awe, as they had been doing for decades.

PBS had great series in the day, including *Eyes on the Prize* and *The Jewel of the Crown*.

At a PBS event at the Ritz Hotel bar in Boston, the venerable British star Alistair Cooke was promoting a show. "Mr. Cooke, can you answer a few questions?" I asked.

He replied to me, with some alarm, "Yes, I will, but right now please stand between me and the crowd. I am about to choke if I don't drink this glass of water." The much-loved icon survived.

After several years of being a TV editor, I became a TV reporter and columnist. This was good because I was not a good editor. I would much rather write than produce pages.

As an editor, planning was not one of my skills. Nor was proofing pages. Deadlines were met, but I was always rushing to get pages to the composing room. I wanted to be out of the office, meeting people and traveling to locations.

One educational junket was to Charleston, S.C., where the miniseries *North and South* was being filmed. Stars included Patrick Swayze, Ken Read, Kirstie Alley, and many others. Stars were dressed in period attire and several media parties were in mansions and venerable hotels in the Low Country.

One day the production's PR team took us to a "real" plantation outside of Charleston. Though slavery had ended more than a century earlier, it was shocking to see Blacks actors huddled in front of tawdry shacks while waiting for the shooting that day.

We later were permitted to enter these shacks, which were authentically recreated. It was appalling to see how the enslaved lived. These "slaves" were dressed in rags and the free-loading media breezed through like so many gawking tourists. In 2025, producers could not permit such insensitive PR scenarios.

Here's another scene from the TV beat: a press tour to the Playboy Mansion. Hefner and the crowd were launching a new series, and some scribes signed up to go to the mansion. The fenced-in grounds were gorgeous and replete with wildlife. The gardens were exquisite. And after a brief walking tour, a half-dozen male dreamers arrived at the Grotto. This was a swimming pool enclosed in a cave where many photo shoots had taken place. When the PR lady asked if we wanted to continue to the "set" on the other side of the grotto, the male heads nodded. But there we found only the show's producers and directors—and they were fully clothed.

A press event in New York was shocking in a different way. NBC had made a miniseries of *Fatal Vision*, based on the Joe McGinness book that focused on the murder of the wife and children of Dr. Jeffrey MacDonald in Fort Bragg, N.C. The well-staged drama starred Gary Cole, Karl Malden, Eva Marie Saint, and examined the story of the bloody 1970 slayings. Dr. MacDonald was convicted of the crime.

At a publicity event in a Manhattan steakhouse, the parents of the deceased young mother had been invited to attend a dinner where the movie would be discussed. But the realism was too much. The parents of the young mother were unable to listen to the "objective" questions from the media as the gruesome slayings were discussed.

MacDonald has been in prison for many years. McGinness became a national figure in the media for his "unorthodox" approach in the book. MacDonald had invited him to come to North Carolina, with the belief that the author would write a story favorable to the doctor.

But McGinness concluded that MacDonald was guilty. He said as much in the book, which undermined the doctor's PR attempt to escape incarceration. The McGinness approach of "betraying" his source was enormously controversial in media circles.

The position of television columnist at the *Boston Herald* provided many subjects to write about. Of the many positions that I have held, it ranks as the most stimulating. Certainly, it involved the most travel and exposure for a humble introvert from Jersey.

The newspaper industry itself may have been fun, but it was not benign. In 1990, I was replaced. For a half-dozen years, I had a great job at the *Herald*. Until I didn't.

What had happened was this: Rupert Murdoch had just purchased TV Guide. And he recruited the TV columnist for *USA Today*, Monica Collins, to be the lead TV writer at the *Herald*.

I had just been given a 15 percent raise. I had received excellent performance reports from superiors, but Rupert thought that Monica, a "national name," could be an asset for both the *Herald* and TV Guide.

I wasn't fired. A menial job on the night news desk was offered. But the position proffered was the same kind as in New Orleans. I was devastated, and perhaps rushed into a bad decision. I left the newspaper.

Perhaps editors Ken Chandler and Alan Eisner were relieved that I left quietly. But able employees were pushed out of this organization frequently.

Herald managers offered me five months' severance pay with a guarantee of unemployment compensation ($645 per week, for a year).

This was a decision I might not repeat. But I was too shocked, and hurt, to stay.

It probably would not have mattered. The newspaper business was changing, and the *Herald* started laying off staffers in the '90s. Indeed, this was my wake-up call to the fact the newspaper industry was declining.

The Boston Globe in 2019 ran a story that stated that since 2000, the newspaper industry had lost more jobs than the coal business, the steel industry, or commercial fishing. Coal? We did worse than coal, a polluting, death-defying enterprise that many Americans would like to outlaw?

During my career as a full-time journalist from 1970 to 2017, many newsrooms declined. My first daily newspaper in Maine, the *Biddeford-Saco Journal,* was shut down without warning a couple years ago. Two weekly newspapers for which I wrote are defunct, *Kitchenware News* (with a national readership) and *Mass High Tech* (a regional publication).

As of 2020, U.S. newspaper employment had fallen by 55 percent since 2000, from 424,000 people to 183,300 in mid-2016, according to the Bureau of Labor Statistics.

After leaving the *Herald*, I tried to catch on with public relations agencies in Boston. The PR agency business is about selling your invisible product and then holding the hand of the client. No offers were extended.

I started a radio show about television called *TubeTalk*. But radio was having a harder time than newspapers. That ended after a few months.

It was 1990. Full-time jobs in the field were scarce. I applied to be a TV columnist for metro newspapers around the country. Applications for reporter, columnist, and even copy editor went out to all sorts of publications. But the industry was shedding jobs, not offering them.

There was a position in Waterville, Maine. My old mentor, Bob Moorehead, was now the publisher of *The Morning Sentinel* there. He wanted a new editor. Actually, he recruited me.

I left the *Boston Herald* in late 1989. I joined *The Morning Sentinel* in July 1990. In that year, I paid to see a mental health therapist. The question, what is going to happen?

Vicki was flexible. She rolled with disappointment. On televised awards shows, spouses are often thanked for their support. Vicki has been a great supporter on the numerous occasions when I was not collecting awards.

In 1990, Vicki worked part-time as a stringer for McGraw-Hill and other publications. At that point, she did not want a career. She was more interested in bringing up the children in Newburyport. She was a very dynamic personality and became the president of the Newburyport parent-teacher organization.

She also wrote art and entertainment stories for local newspapers. She and her mother, Virginia Lawson, visiting from Memphis, met conductor Leonard Bernstein at Tanglewood one summer. They both almost perished from delight.

Vicki loved Newburyport. The kids loved Newburyport. I loved it. I had joined a tennis club, and I had many friends. Vicki had many friends. The kids had many friends. It was perfect. But I didn't have a job. I moved to Waterville.

I say "I," because the Hendrickson family didn't move immediately. I worked in Waterville during the week and came home on weekends. Round trip, it's about 300 miles. I had a small apartment in Skowhegan, which was owned by the newspaper. It was rent free.

I didn't want to move everyone without being sure the job would work out. After a year, it seemed everything was fine. So, we moved. The family departed wonderful Newburyport in August 1991. We bought a pleasant five-bedroom house in Waterville (population 15,000, host to Colby College) overlooking a park in August.

We settled in. And then in March 1992, I was laid off.

The Morning Sentinel suddenly merged with *The Kennebec Journal*, in nearby Augusta. The top staffers in Waterville lost their jobs, including Bob Moorehead. Including me. Again, a trip to see a mental health counselor. Same question: Why couldn't I keep a job? What would happen?

By then, Vicki had landed a job as a sales executive with public television in Bangor. And so, we weren't doomed.

I was able to rejoin the *Press Herald* in Portland. Because I had done well there a decade earlier, editor Lou Ureneck hired me as a permanent, part-time reporter. It was forty hours per week, though there were no guarantees that this would last.

My shift was from 4 p.m. to midnight on the news desk. News briefs, simple stories, and the police beat. It was the worst job in the newsroom. Plus, it was

80 miles to Portland. One way, five days a week. Holiday, weekends. I logged as many hours as possible. I was scared.

Vicki's journey from Waterville to Bangor was 55 miles, one way, every day. We were really stretched. And during icy Maine winters, commuting was hazardous.

When I see cheery job counselors and motivational speakers repeat the phrase, "Take risks," I chuckle without mirth. Risks had been taken. As a result, I was out of work and my family was vulnerable. In 1991, I had fallen from the high wire. Again.

Several *Press Herald* colleagues who had known me from my glory days would see me in the newsroom and ask, "You used to be Dyke Hendrickson, didn't you? What happened?"

I had left the Portland newsroom in 1981 as an award-winning luminary, and I returned to take the lowest job in the newsroom. But I went in every day, collecting a regular paycheck and looking for another job.

Vicki would grow to hate Waterville. Again, she headed the local parent-teacher organization, but the community was unexciting. It was a former mill town that was never redeveloped. If it hadn't had Colby College within its borders, it would be a very discouraging place. Bill Cosby spoke at a graduation there and asked the proud parents and graduates: "How did you ever find this place?"

Vicki always has had a great deal of energy and good cheer. She prevailed. As a result, our family has prevailed. She subscribed to the symphony in Boston and would drive down every few months for performances (four hours each way). She attended cultural events in Bangor after work. She invited her Memphis-based mother to Waterville for extended visits.

The kids adjusted. Leslie did well in high school and was named to the National Honor Society after her junior year. She was such a good student; she was permitted to take several courses at Colby. Leslie played on the varsity tennis team. And she was chosen to be a page in the U.S. Senate by Sen. George Mitchell, who is from Waterville. In Washington, she thrived. Leslie was elected by other pages to give the farewell address for her class. We traveled to the Senate for her presentation, and it remains one of the proudest moments of my life.

Drew also did very well. His marks were excellent, and he was a state junior champion in tennis, which would not have happened in Massachusetts. He had many friends.

We did a lot together. We went camping on our land in nearby New Sharon. We went canoeing; we fished. Because I had a press pass through my ski column with the *Maine Sunday Telegram*, we often went skiing. In Maine, you have to drive many miles to get to recreational events. Because we spent so much time in the car together, the kids and I talked for hours. I value this odd upside—conversation—that developed in a troubled period in our lives. Plus, the kids developed into great tennis players and terrific skiers.

The anguish I am describing now sounds like a first world problem. But for much of the early '90s, I thought I had doomed the family. Vicki wanted to return to Massachusetts, hopefully to Newburyport.

We knew we would move at some point. For that reason, we had Drew apply to Milton Academy. This is one of the most distinguished prep schools in the country. Ted Kennedy and Bobby Kennedy went there, as did former Massachusetts Gov. Deval Patrick. The list could go on for many column inches.

We had friends from Newburyport, Tom and Fran Flaherty, who were on the staff at Milton. We felt if Drew went to Milton, he would be in school when we moved back to Massachusetts. Drew was a good student and a state tennis champion. The staffer who interviewed him was Frank Millet, a legendary "Mr. Chips" character who coached tennis and squash at Milton for decades.

When Mr. Millett asked Drew how long he had been playing tennis, Drew replied, "Since I was in swaddling clothes." Drew was accepted.

Drew had a tough time adjusting. His peers were among the smartest in the country. Many graduating seniors go to Ivy League universities. He had had a good education, but those who attended Milton were great students.

But Drew prevailed. By his senior year, he was captain of the tennis and basketball teams. He was a starter on the undefeated football team. He was a B student at a Class A prep school. He learned a great deal at Milton and made many friends. Today his school friends are from Milton, not the University of New Hampshire, the college from which he graduated.

While we were in Waterville, Drew and I attended a weekend seminar where tennis players could be certified to teach tennis. The organization was the National Professional Tennis Registry, based in Hilton Head, S.C. Drew, sixteen, earned a junior credential.

Drew's "license" enabled him to get his first teaching job at the Farm Neck Club on Martha's Vineyard. He taught there for numerous summers making good money. Later, this background helped him get a full-time job at Tenacity in Boston, a well-funded organization that brings tennis and tutoring to the inner city. His teaching certificate got him started in the tennis industry and will serve him for a lifetime. By 2025, he had started All Court Enrichment, his own tennis-and-tutoring program in Somerville and Medford, Massachusetts.

Drew was accepted at Emory University, his first choice. He later transferred to the University of New Hampshire. He earned a master's degree from Union Theological Seminary in New York. Leslie was accepted at the college of her choice, St. John's College in Annapolis and Santa Fe. She earned a master's from Columbia Journalism School. They are thriving, making their father feel very relieved as he enters his dotage.

After leaving the *Press Herald* in about 1993, jobs as editor on small weekly publications followed. I was editor of *Kitchenware News* in Yarmouth, Maine, and editor of the *Woburn Advocate* in Woburn, Massachusetts.

At that point, any job was appreciated.

The newspaper field was diminishing. But major stories were still broken by the print media. Though it is forgotten now, much of the early reporting on the Bill Clinton-Monica Lewinsky saga was done by *Newsweek* and *The Washington Post*.

14

The Hendricksons Rally

In the late '90s, technology was a hot field in the Hub. I was a reporter for *Mass High Tech*, a sister newspaper to the *Boston Business Journal*. *MHT* went out of business years ago, but it had a dynamic life for about a decade.

Getting that job was the break the Hendricksons needed to return to Newburyport. As usual, the money was minimal. It paid $30,000 per year (in 1996), which is what I was making fifteen years earlier! We bought a modest house in 1998 in Newburyport for $190,000. It was probably the last house sold for under $200,000 in this desirable community.

What happened was this: Vicki was visiting friends in Newburyport when she saw an elderly couple putting a "For Sale" sign on their lawn. They were selling the residence themselves. It was on Low Street, which is the same street where we lived from 1985–1992. Vicki hit the brakes and made an offer on the spot. The owners were surprised, but they accepted. They got their price, and they would not have to pay commission to a broker.

Returning to Newburyport has been a gift. Since returning in 1998, Vicki has become a star. She earned a master's degree in education from the University of New Hampshire. After that, she founded the Newburyport Adult Education program. It has been a vital part of community life for close to two decades.

Vicki also founded the Newburyport Literary Festival, which has been rated among the best in New England. In recent years she has been honored by the Massachusetts State House for community service, and by the city of Newburyport for being the top educator of the year. The Greater Newburyport Chamber of Commerce lauded her as a Citizen of the Year.

15

The Story of Technology

The job at *Mass High Tech* turned out to be exciting, educational, and it led to a well-paying public relations post with Massachusetts General Hospital (2006–2009). But that is getting ahead of the story.

Obtaining a job as a technology reporter at this point reflects my theory that Boomers have had many opportunities in our lifetimes. I was fifty-one, yet I was given the chance to cover a new medium known as the internet. Mainstream media often carries bad news stories about unemployment, eviction, and economic despair. But the U.S. has an incredibly vibrant economy. From out of nowhere, industries like online communication and wireless technology developed rapidly. Millions of jobs were created, even as many Americans were left behind.

The internet—as opposed to the World Wide Web—was created in the late '60s by several top universities working with federal authorities. National leaders wanted a communications system should the country come under attack.

In the mid-'90s, the notion of the internet was expanded into the World Wide Web. This technology permitted "regular people" to have access to a revolutionary communications tool. Tim Berners-Lee, a British mathematician who settled at MIT, is credited with developing the World Wide Web in about 1989.

Many other technologies were soon introduced. In 1993, Marc Andreesen developed Mosaic, later called Netscape. His work is credited with sparking the internet boom of the 1990s. Mark Zuckerberg, an undergraduate at Harvard, was another key player. He and others created Facebook. A movie titled *The Social Media* focused on how the technology championed by undergrads came to influence the world.

MIT and Harvard were at the head of this parade in the late '90s. Stanford, too, was a leader. Hundreds of scientists came to Cambridge to learn more. It soon became acknowledged that this technology would change the world.

Mass High Tech was a weekly publication that was in the middle of this early boom. We had four reporters, four salespeople, two editors, a publisher, and a part-time photographer.

We wrote stories about young entrepreneurs who started hardware and software companies. We put on seminars and retreats about how to succeed in electronic commerce. Some of our largest advertisers were banks, accounting companies and investment firms that wanted to learn which fledgling companies merited investment.

Our modest little weekly became the place to go for information about start-ups and new technology. *The Boston Globe*, in the early years, was too high and mighty to cover companies just getting started. The *Herald*'s readership was more entertained by murder and pro sports.

Mass High Tech gained advertisers so fast the young, energetic staff could hardly keep up with demand. We went from a sixteen-page black-and-white throwaway to a color product often featuring forty-eight or sixty-four pages.

Our office was small, and the reporters could hear the excited advertising salespeople through the cheap cubicles. Frequently, a sales staffer would take a cold call and a few minutes later she would have a full-page ad for the next issue.

The industry was growing quickly, and each reporter wrote about five stories a week about promising companies. An online company like Amazon, created in 1997, grew to 1 million employees by 2021. Scores of companies in the Boston area became national enterprises. Thousands of investors, private and institutional, made piles of money by investing in tech companies.

I went to many events at MIT and Harvard where I heard tech execs talk about their new companies. One early company I wrote about was Akamai Technologies.

Akamai is a global company, providing web and internet security services. Akamai's Intelligent Edge Platform is one of the world's largest distributed computing platforms. Its technology enables the web to operate quickly even when many users have signed on.

This company has a larger-than-life backstory that is anchored in personal disaster. One of its founders, Danny Lewin, was killed on an airplane during the terrorist attacks on September 11, 2001. Lewin was emerging as one of the brilliant stars of the online world, East Coast version, when he died.

Upon receiving an undergraduate degree in 1995 in Israel, where he had grown up, he began graduate studies at MIT in 1996. He and his advisor, Professor Tom Leighton, developed an innovative algorithm for optimizing internet traffic. These algorithms became the basis for the company that the two founded in 1998. Lewin served as the company's technologist and a board member, and he achieved great wealth during the height of the internet boom.

But he died on September 11. There is a small square in Cambridge that is named after him. Board leader Tom Leighton still tears up when talking about Lewin and the early days of the company. I suspect a Netflix documentary is being made of this provocative story.

Another company that grew quickly was CMGI, which offered online business solutions. It had been a collegiate book publisher and distributor before the arrival of online communication. I interviewed CEO David Wetherell in about 1997, and he said, "I guess the biggest use of the web is pornography, but eventually doing business online will also be worth billions." He was correct on both counts.

CMGI sprinted to the lead of media stature in the late '90s. Its prominence and its financial resources were so great that the new football stadium for the New England Patriots was to be named CMGI Field. But when the tech bust devastated many companies in 2001, CMGI all but disappeared. Gillette won the naming rights to the football stadium. Wetherell faded away.

My job included travel to national tech conferences in San Francisco and New York. Other tech retreats took place on Nantucket and Cape Cod. Once a year, tech leaders retreated to Camden, Maine, to discuss new ideas and promising markets.

Then-Maine Gov. Angus King was in Camden in the late '90s when he announced his plan to make sure every middle-school student in Maine had a lap-top computer. He was ahead of the curve in realizing that students who were not wealthy needed to stay abreast of new learning applications. He is now a U.S. senator who runs as an Independent.

Though Silicon Valley in California is recognized as ground zero for the tech boom, the Boston-Cambridge area was also on fire in the late '90s. The West Coast has Stanford and Berkeley, but the MIT-Harvard tandem also produces many provocative companies.

In the late '90s, social events hosted by tech entrepreneurs were thrown on the roof of the Prudential Center. Yachts were rented for parties on Boston Harbor. The best restaurants were commandeered for private parties thrown for investors, executives and the media. I thrived in this position, perhaps because I can always find a "professional connection" to a party.

Innovation was a must for the technological crowd. MIT launched an innovation competition, the "MIT $50K," that became the talk of the country. At this annual event, student teams of four or five would present their business plans to professors and investors. Some "business plans" developed into viable companies. The tech industry was on fire with financial success and scientific achievement.

One day Bill Gates was at Harvard to make a donation and get an honorary degree. Gates, who left Harvard before graduating, said with a grin, "Now that I am going into a new career [philanthropy], I suppose it's time for me to have a degree."

The Microsoft founder did something very thoughtful at a small seminar there. He was to deliver a PowerPoint presentation explaining some new company technology. A young student technician was having trouble starting the program. When Gates drifted over to see what was wrong, the nervous student became unhinged that the great Gates was looking over his shoulder.

Gates realized this and went to an opposite corner of the room to talk to students and investors. With Gates gone, the young technician was able to calm down and launch the program.

At an innovation conference at MIT in 1999, Vice President Al Gore was the speaker. The media had indicated that Gore was stiff and boring, but this Harvard graduate was among the most congenial speakers on the scene. "I am here to address the rumors," Gore smiled. "Yes, I invented the Internet." He joked about his former roommate, actor Tommy Lee Jones. Gore was loose and amusing.

Actor Terri Garr spoke at a medical conference. She started soberly, "My name is Terri Garr, and I am an alcoholic." Then she suddenly began shuffling papers on the podium. "Wait!" she cried. "Wrong speech! My name is Terri Garr and I am here to speak about Parkinson's disease." That brought a good laugh, even at 9 in the morning.

When covering newsmakers at MIT, Harvard, Boston University, Northeastern, and other schools, I relayed a lot of information. Because the internet was new and unknown, my coverage was followed by many readers in the Boston area.

From 1998 to the tech crash in 2001, the Boston-Cambridge market was awash in money. Companies wanted to invest. Individuals wanted to cash out.

At a tech luncheon in downtown Boston, it became evident that investors at every level were succeeding. Usually, the restaurant offered valet parking. But no attendant came out. The manager later said that the attendant's Internet stocks were going wild, and he had quit to become a day trader.

On another occasion, a middle-aged high school teacher visiting from Florida heard the tech pitch of one of his former students who was leaving Harvard to start a new company. The excited teacher decided to quit his job on the spot to join his ex-student's company. A few days later, his wife insisted that he return to his tenured post as a math teacher. He listened to her, and went back to the high school classroom

The MIT-Harvard community was a go-to place for investment companies developing e-commerce, wireless communications and websites that sold over the web. Investment in start-ups was a much-publicized activity. Northeastern, Boston University, Tufts, and other schools in the area also developed programs that produced small companies.

So much money was flying around it was difficult to resist offers that sounded tempting. So, I joined a start-up.

I had become friendly with the founder of a tech start-up called Wired Empire. His name was Ed Mullen, and offered me a job as public relations director. The salary was $65,000 per year. And I would get 1,000 shares of stock. I was making about $40,000 at this time. Many of the young newsmakers I wrote about were becoming rich. This seemed to be my chance. I took the job, leaving *Mass High Tech* after about five years.

Wired Empire was creating an online purchasing system for big companies. It had secured about $10 million from an anonymous source. Levi's jeans company was supposedly an early client.

But at Wired Empire's plush offices, there was nothing to do. There were no press releases to write, no journalists to pitch to generate publicity. Was there really a product?

In the newspaper world, you write at least one story a day. There is always something to do. At the end of the day, you leave knowing you have produced something. In this PR job, there were no assignments or specific goals. You went to meetings; you planned to attend conferences. On numerous days, eight-hour shifts were spent without doing anything but going to meetings.

A vice president of communications was my direct superior. He didn't have anything to do either. He set up meetings, he took meetings, he networked with old friends from business school. Many new employees didn't know if there actually was a product such as a novel software app. It didn't seem to matter. There was a saying in the business that suggested a company could "Fake it until you make it." We seemed to be doing that.

I went to conferences in San Francisco, Toronto, and New York. I "worked the booth" as Wired Empire tried to get visibility in the red-hot world of e-commerce. We ramped up to about thirty-two employees. Our top executives continued to seek more investment money. I eventually wrote pamphlets and web advertising for Wired Empire's "special technology." But we had no sales, and no further investment that I knew of.

Once I called Levi's headquarters to "get to know" our clients. I thought I could write a "client testimonial" to promote Wired Empire. But my contact at Levi's said her company did not have a contract with us. They wanted us to remove their name from our literature. Bad sign: Big client disavows contract.

We could hire employees, acquire new office space, and "talk the talk," but we did not have clients or revenue. There didn't seem to be an actual product. And it occurred to me that 1,000 shares of nothing is still nothing.

At about that time (*circa* 2001), there was a job opening at *Mass High Tech*. I returned. They were making a lot of money and offered me $65,000 upon my return. I had been very fortunate to return to a stable job with benefits. Wired Empire folded about a year later.

In my new incarnation, biotech, medical devices, and healthcare made up my beat. The Boston area has dozens of hospitals, and it was a fertile market for ideas that melded medicine and online technology.

One of the fastest growing businesses was athenahealth, started by Jonathan Bush, the likable young cousin of President George W. Bush. Jonathan Bush headed a fledgling firm that had five employees. Its technology provided an application to medium-sized businesses for billing, appointments, and communication. It raised $10 million in 2000 and ramped up to hundreds of employees by the time Bush left as CEO in 2018. Jonathan Bush, a highly visible executive who could generate much publicity for the company, made millions after his firm was purchased by a larger competitor.

About a year after I returned to *Mass High Tech*, I was named the editor of that publication. Salary was $75,000 per year. It was a high visibility post, and initially all went well. One of my memorable moments came the week after the terrorist attacks of September 11, 2001. Under my direction, our staff provided profiles with photos of all Boston tech-area personnel who had lost their lives. It was a moving, well-planned tribute.

Because *Mass High Tech* was doing so well, the tiny publication was purchased by American City Business Journals. ACBJ, based in Charlotte, N.C., owned the *Boston Business Journal.* It also owned other business pubs, including weeklies in San Francisco, Atlanta, and Charlotte.

The ACBJ executives chose *BBJ* publisher Mike Olivieri to launch tech journals in other cities where it owned a business journal. As the year 2000 emerged, high-tech weeklies were launched in Washington, Denver, Houston, and a couple other cities.

I was asked to become the editor of the new tech journal in Washington. Mike and I flew to D.C. to get a sense of the market. I did not take the job. It was fortunate I declined because after the tech bust of 2001, all these fledgling newspapers failed. Mike went 0 for 5.

Perhaps because of his frustration, he started lambasting me. I was upbraided for a typo in a headline or a poorly designed page. I did not write the headlines, but I was responsible for errors. I had once been a star, but now I was in the doghouse.

The tension that I felt resulted in a case of Bell's palsy. One morning I woke up, and I couldn't open my left eye. That side of my face seemed paralyzed. I went to the doctor and learned that it is a condition often brought on by tension. At the end of the week, I resigned as editor.

Since the job of covering online media had been filled, I took the reporter job of covering medical innovation and biotech. I knew very little about this field. But it was another opportunity coming my way.

The Boston-Cambridge market was the most dynamic in the country when it came to medical innovation. Its research universities include MIT, Harvard, Tufts, and BU. Research was done around the clock. Federal research grants were announced by some institution almost every day.

Teaching hospitals associated with Harvard are among the best in the world, including Massachusetts General Hospital, New England Baptist Hospital, Beth-Israel Deaconess Hospital, and others.

Brilliant scientists were developing fast-growing companies. Genzyme and Biogen were among the top medical companies in the world as they became leaders in "orphan drugs." These are medications that are designed for a small population, and companies are permitted to develop their product without industry competition.

Many research nonprofits were developed at this time. The Broad Institute associated with MIT was launched to study DNA and other unraveling mysteries with $100 million in investment money. I covered Alkermes, Inc., when it had only a dozen employees. Its medication promised to halt excess and drug abuse with just one shot per month. The company was sold and resold, and everyone on the ground floor made millions.

In print journalism, newspapers were producing big stories but not making much money. Owners talked about layoffs, not profits.

Yet the *Globe* earned national attention by breaking stories about the Catholic Church's enabling sexual abuse of minors. Many priests had had sex with boys and girls over the decades, and the church had kept this from the public. In addition, cardinals and bishops had reassigned guilty priests so they arrived in new parishes with no warning.

Editor Marty Baron, who is Jewish and had not grown up in Boston, managed this project with notable persistence. The newspaper won the Pulitzer Prize, and the project was turned into the moved *Spotlight*. The film won the Academy Award for Best Picture in 2016.

Baron's insistence that the team publish story after story was an effective means of stressing the depth of the abuse. Political leaders could not ignore the provocative series. Eventually, the church had to acknowledge these crimes, and Catholic leaders have been resigning in markets all over the world ever since.

16

Biotech: A Story of Remarkable Science

At the turn of the twenty-first century, the medical sector was awash in money. Investors were looking for the next Viagra. Pharma execs were seeking small start-ups to determine if they were worth buying. Think tanks like Forrester and McKinsey would comb the marketplace, looking for the new-new thing so they could lecture execs on what was happening at the ground-roots level.

By early 2006, life was good for the Hendricksons. The children had graduated college, and Vicki was emerging as a star of both Adult Education and the Newburyport Literary Festival. In addition to her jobs, she took about $100,000 out of our modest split-level house to reform it into an attractive residence. And she launched a massive garden.

Things were going so well that Fate announced it was time for our own Dyke Hendrickson to get knocked off his perch again.

In 2006, a new editor came aboard at *Mass High Tech*. He was about twenty-eight; he looked fourteen. He was tiny. He did not like my work. I had a hard time being reverential about his presence. Also, I was getting bored. Enthusiasm and curiosity evidently cut both ways. I have great curiosity. But after initial contact, I often lost interest in a given subject. I must remember that when I analyze my hot-and-cold career.

I covered most of the young biotech and medical device companies. Unlike the tech companies who could fake it until they make it, the medical firms had to show data and results. Most scientists don't posture or make up story lines. I didn't have as many stories to chase.

Looking back, I could get jobs, but not always hold them. I did not make myself essential to the company. Perhaps I lacked gravitas. Also, it's always a simple matter to replace a reporter. Though an in-house survey said my column was the most read part of *Mass High Tech*, that didn't help me keep a job.

Most editors want to be revered as "The Boss." I did not have much respect for the teen editor. I was the face of the newspaper, and some editors want that role for themselves.

Our pretentious editor wanted me gone. After I left, he went through three more reporters in my beat over the next year. Soon after the newspaper folded.

17

A Good (Short) Story: Partners Healthcare

In late 2006, I was laid off from *Mass High Tech*. I got a generous severance package. It was embarrassing to lose another job, but I was well-positioned. The newspaper industry was fading. The healthcare industry was thriving.

I had hardly had a chance to file my unemployment documents when I was hired by Partners Healthcare as a communications manager. The job paid $80,000 per year, had great health benefits, and was reachable by commuter rail.

Partners Healthcare was the largest medical provider in New England. I worked for a research unit inside Partners known as CIMIT, the Center for the Integration of Medicine and Innovative Technology. Nowadays I say I worked for Massachusetts General Hospital, which was the largest institution within Partners. It is too difficult to explain CIMIT.

CIMIT was a medical incubator that pulled in about $8 million per year in federal funding. It gave small grants to doctors and scientists. For instance, if a Harvard Medical School surgeon had a new technique to remove a gallbladder, he might get $100,000 from CIMIT to launch preliminary tests. If the early research was promising, the team leader would use the data to obtain larger grants for more studies.

CIMIT was well-connected. It had relationships with all the Harvard teaching hospitals, as well MIT, Tufts, BU, and the U.S. Army. To get the job as communications manager, I had to interview with eight different doctors and/or Ph.D. researchers who were associated with CIMIT. Since I had covered medical matters for *Mass High Tech*, this job was a good fit.

One note on interviewing: During my last interview with CIMIT, the executive interviewing me had heard of my college, Franklin and Marshall. His daughter had gone there. This marked the only time in my much-traveled career when an interviewer indicated she had heard of my college. All eight of the medical executives voted to hire me. I interviewed well. It was keeping the jobs that was challenging.

In 2006, I was sixty-one. Great, a well-paying job in a stimulating environment. But again, in this public relations job, there was hardly anything to do!

Working under the vice president of external affairs, I went to meetings. I attended conferences; I helped set up the booth when CIMIT traveled to professional gatherings. But there were many hours of dead time.

Also, most medical professionals doing promising research are not seeking publicity. They want to create a thesis, prove their point, and then have their work reviewed. One of the worst things a communications manager could do is write press releases before the doctor is ready. Research takes time.

There were several stories that I thought would merit media attention.

One young doctor with contacts in Kenya was creating baby incubators from unused Toyota parts. Toyota, with factories in that part of the world, thought such a story would make the company look good. It provided the Harvard-based doctor funding for a project that had great potential. But managers of this intriguing project frustrated me by repeatedly saying it was "too early" to send out a press release.

Another CIMIT-funded researcher had created a facsimile of an injured soldier. It had "real" organs and "moving blood." His plan was to make it available to the military services so their medics-in-training could learn on a "real" body rather than a dummy. CIMIT had got him started, but the researcher wanted no publicity at the time.

As a result of the reticence in the medical research world, I had almost nothing to do. But my boss thought I was doing great. I got a raise every six months and was at $95,000 per year when funding patron Ted Kennedy died. After that, life at CIMIT became difficult.

18

Life Away from the Office: The Cabin, the Literary Festival

In the early 2000s, my avocations were tennis, the cabin in Maine and the Newburyport Literary Festival.

I had always played tennis. In 2008, our local tennis club won the New England team championship in the sixty-and-over category. We played in the 4.0 division, which was classified as moderately advanced.

We went to the national championships in Surprise, Arizona. It was wall-to-wall tennis for a whole weekend. The complex there had more than thirty courts. Vicki went with me. When she got tired of the tennis, she went shopping and sightseeing. One day we drove up to Sedona.

Our team emerged 2-1 and ranked fifth of sixteen teams from different regions of the country. My partner, Dick Canepa, and I were victorious in the one match we played. My career record on the national level remains unblemished: 1-0.

A greater endeavor was building a cabin in Maine. With my grandmother's help in 1968, land on the Sandy River in New Sharon, Maine was purchased. About 18 acres. In 2005, we made plans to build a cabin. I cut out a photo in a book, *The Cabin*. It was a modest dwelling in North Carolina. I "found" my builder from a business card on the bulletin board of the local farm store in New Sharon.

Vicki was not inspired by this project. But we often take separate paths.

Our local builder went into action. He cut down trees, bulldozed the land and put up a one-room cabin about 24 feet by 20 feet. The walls were insulated but not the floor or ceiling. Later, a wood stove for heat and cooking was installed. A well was drilled, and the water was cool and delicious. One asset is the large front porch, upon which we cooked out and imbibed. From this perch, we watched the sunset.

There was, and is, no power. It would have been $10,000 to install it, because the utility company would have had to bring it about 1,000 yards down the road. The project was already costing about $12,000. As a career journalist who had just helped put two kids through college, there wasn't money that would permit such an "extra" as electricity.

It is a three-season retreat. It was on a public road, but the town did not plow to our property. This was a rural version of Catch-22. We were on a public road, but the snowplows didn't get to 103 Flagg. Town officials said that no one was there in the winter. So why plow?

It was uninhabited because we couldn't reach it—there was too much snow. It is still unoccupied in winter. Our wood stove can heat the cabin in the evening, but once the fire dies, the interior can reach the freezing mark. It can get very cold in Maine.

Building the cabin has been a very rewarding experience. The kids and I would walk about 500 yards to the river, which is very clean. There are no houses in sight. We would canoe, fish and swim. When Vicki came, we could go into nearby Farmington, which had a branch of the state university (*circa* 2,000 students) and numerous attractive shops.

We still have the cabin. It is still without power. The well provides wonderful water, and the outhouse has never failed us. It is a good retreat for writing books; Leslie and Drew have both used it with friends and/or family. In 2020, it was deeded to the children.

Another notable development in the twenty-first century was the arrival of the Newburyport Literary Festival. Vicki started it as a means of encouraging people to read more. She had spent twenty years in the TV business, but what she believed in was books.

The festival makes for a busy weekend. Before Covid, close to seventy authors would appear in a dozen venues. Churches were used, as was City Hall and a municipal performing venue known as the Firehouse Center for the Arts.

One of the most prominent authors to participate was Sen. George Mitchell, who came in 2017. His book was *The Negotiator*. I narrated the presentation from the stage of the Firehouse Auditorium. Mitchell discussed his renowned effort to bring peace to Northern Ireland. What a success story. Close to 200 listened intently, and he signed seventy-eight books following his hour-long presentation.

But before starting, he praised my book, *Quiet Presence: Stories of Franco-Americans in New England*. Though it came out in 1980, he said it was one of the most valuable books he had read because it profiled the lives of mill workers in communities like Waterville, where he grew up.

What a nice thing to say! He may have been blowing smoke, but if so, I appreciated these second-hand fumes.

Another appearance that I narrated was that of Tess Gerritsen, one of the most successful fiction writers in the country. She is a native of Hawaii, a medical doctor, and she has settled in scenic Camden, Maine, to raise a family and write murder mysteries with medical insight. A pair of her characters found their way into a TV series, *Rizzoli and Isles*. It ran for almost a decade, which is an incredible feat in that industry.

One question was, "Did you do much research for your mystery involving NASA?" She had written a script. Later, a movie was released that appeared to follow her story. It was titled *Gravity*. It was a high-profile production that starred Sandra Bullock and George Clooney.

Tess is a mild-mannered novelist, but she bristled when I mentioned this topic. She said:

> I spent more than a year talking to NASA people, visiting sites and learning about the space program.
>
> And then this movie comes out titled, *Gravity*, with George Clooney and Sandra Bullock.
>
> That was my idea. When my lawyer called the producers, they said they knew nothing about my proposal. They said they had a Hollywood writer do a little research on the Internet and then some script doctors to put the screenplay together.
>
> I was furious. I still am. I spent months researching that and my work was stolen. I am still suing.

Another memorable interview was with Rachel Slade who wrote the book *Into the Raging Sea*. She is a Boston-area writer, now affiliated with *The Boston Globe*. Rachel got one of the great nautical scoops of recent years and turned it into a book.

The story: *El Faro*, an 800-foot tanker, sank during a storm between St. Petersburg, Florida, and Puerto Rico in 2015. The captain was very slow in calling for help and the vessel went down before the Coast Guard could even mount a rescue. All thirty-three aboard were lost.

The ship sank in 15,000 feet of water. But an unmanned sub was able to retrieve the "black box." Known mostly from the airline industry, the black box is an indestructible data recorder secured on the bridge of the vessel.

Slade heard that the black box was undamaged. She requested to be present when the conversation from the final hours on the bridge were replayed. The sound was excellent—and revealing. She knew she had a huge story.

The recording depicted junior officers recognizing the danger the ship was in hours before the captain acted. They wanted to change course, but the captain demurred. When they got into 60-foot seas, they wanted the captain to come to the bridge. But he was sleeping. Because she had access to the conversation in the final excruciating hours, her book was a sensation. It was being made into a TV series in 2022.

Added tangent: a spurned captain. One questioner at my session elicited the assertion that the captain's romantic advances had been spurned by a junior female officer. Thereafter, he would not talk to her or communicate with her on the bridge. She was on duty during the storm. It is troubling to think that his reluctance to communicate with her was a cause of the disaster.

Mel Allen, editor of *Yankee* magazine who I had known in Portland, helped land her for the festival. She had written a lengthy story on the disaster for *Yankee*.

Writers honored over the years by the festival include abolitionist scribe William Lloyd Garrison and Pulitzer Prize-winner John Marquand, both natives of

Newburyport. Other prominent writers who have participated at the festival include Richard Russo, Elizabeth Strout, Andre Dubus III, Joyce Maynard, Anita Shreve, Wally Lamb, Rina Espaillat, Bob Ryan, Bill Lee, and Peter Guralnick.

Regarding books, reading is a great hobby. Like many seniors, I have read (or listened to) thousands in a lifetime. At least half of them have been audiobooks.

The most provocative book for me was *Guns, Germs and Steel* by Jared Diamond (1997).

Those who study history wonder why some civilizations thrive and others are exploited. How did English-based colonialism succeed in dominating much of the world, including North America. And how did small Spanish forces subjugate massive native civilizations in Mexico and South America?

Diamond suggests it was because of geography, science, and luck. European groups had acquired immunities to diseases in earlier centuries. They could arrive and conquer. In America, for instance, many more native Americans died of disease than in warfare.

He suggested that stable societies enabled communities to develop science that resulted not only in medicine but in knives, guns and transportation systems. The concept of Christianity encouraged achievement.

In the case of the United States, its geography meant that it was never invaded. Not many nations have that advantage.

Regarding writers, my favorites include John Grisham, Michael Connelly, Linda Fairstein, Elmore Leonard, Jill Lepore, David McCullough, and Michael Lewis. A guilty pleasure is Stuart Woods.

A favorite historian is Doris Kearns Goodwin. I've read *Team of Rivals* twenty-five times, and histories of the Roosevelts at least a dozen times. More books are consumed as audio books than those in hard copy.

Listening to books on tape started when my car traveled from Pass Christian to New Orleans (65 miles). Later, it was Waterville to Portland (80 miles). And now, it is a three-hour ride from Newburyport to our cabin in New Sharon. I would have fallen asleep at the wheel long ago if I had not had a book to entertain me.

But back to my checkered career. In 2009, about ten of us were laid off at CIMIT. Ted Kennedy was gone and so was the $8 million in funding that he delivered each year. New managers wanted to spend less.

There was a generous severance package and unemployment benefits to allay the familiar disappointment. As I looked for jobs, I wrote a book, *Franco-Americans of Maine*, my third tome. In 2005, I had written a novel titled *Last Night in Hollywood*, based on my experiences in covering the TV industry in Hollywood. Several publishers showed interest, but none offered me a contract. I published that myself.

But here it was again, losing a job. In 2009, I was sixty-four. When entering the employment world after college, I could never have expected to lose so many jobs. None of my peers have had so many positions.

19

Back to the Future: Return to Local Newspapers

In about 2011, I began freelancing for local newspapers. Vicki was pleased with her work in the Adult Education and Community Education division of the Newburyport School Department. The kids had launched and were out of the house. I returned to daily newspapers because I needed something to do.

I was sixty-six, but newspapers needed reporters. Not many young people were entering this doomed profession. *The Gloucester Daily Times* hired me. This well-known fishing community is about 25 miles from Newburyport.

And in 2012, *The Daily News* in Newburyport offered me a job.

The Gloucester and Newburyport papers were owned by the same chain. John Macone, the editor in Newburyport, knew my work because the Gloucester paper arrived in his office every day. And I had written well-regarded freelance stories for him.

So, at the age of sixty-six, my job was covering city hall, just like in Petaluma in 1970 (when I was twenty-five).

The salary was low—$32,000 per year. Nothing new about low salaries in journalism. But now there were Social Security payments coming in and two small pensions to enhance this pitiful sum.

Newburyport is a dynamic small community. It is located at the confluence of the Merrimack River and the Atlantic Ocean. Nearby Plum Island, a barrier island about 5 miles east of Newburyport, hosts the Parker River National Wildlife Refuge. It offers 7 miles of wild beachfront that is administered by federal officials. Birds, animals, and fish abound.

Working at *The Daily News* was rewarding. Unlike fields of biotech or computer engineering that I had covered without personal expertise, I understood city hall. My other beat was the waterfront. We had a small fishing industry and a very large summer boating environment.

Because Newburyport is a desirable community, some development company was always trying to bend the rules to put a condominium community on the river or houses along the ocean. This was a conflict over community growth, which I had covered many times. *The Daily News* was a comfortable fit in a beautiful community where we lived.

I liked working at *The Daily News*. Though our staff of sixteen was whittled down to eight because of budget cuts and/or transfers, the day-by-day work was rewarding.

One reason the job was appealing was that each staffer got six weeks off per year. Two were from vacation, and four were from furlough. The newspaper chain was losing money and wanted to cut the amount they paid to reporters.

Four weeks off was great, even if those days were unpaid. In two successive years, I flew to Palm Springs, Calif., to watch the Indian Wells pro tennis tournament. One year Drew joined me, and the following year Leslie came. We had a great time. It was like going to Disney World again, though now it wasn't free.

We went to New York to watch the U.S. Open. During one spring we went to Paris, and we saw the French Open as well as the museums.

With six weeks off, I also went to Florida each spring to see my sister, Dale. She and her husband, Dick Magee, took a condo on the ocean each February in New Smyrna Beach on the Atlantic side. They had two bedrooms, so it was free. I rented a car each year and soon found a great tennis club that welcomed snowbirds. I have gone there for ten winters, and it has made the season more bearable.

20

Still in Newspapers, also Writing Books

My third trimester has been about Newburyport. We moved here in 1998, and in this seaside community there has been much to write about. One source of stories was the ongoing erosion activity at Plum Island.

In recent years, wealthy people have been building houses on the dunes along the northern sector of the island. Many are close to the high tide mark. The ocean takes a few more feet from the shoreline each year.

People keep building because the view is spectacular. An observer coming from a different planet, or even a landlocked state like Kansas, might say, "This is a barrier island. Why do they build so close to the sea?" Or "Why do the local building inspectors give permits for edifices that will likely be pummeled by the rising, ferocious sea?"

Good questions. Every year houses are damaged by the surf. In about 2015, six homes were destroyed, and two dozen condemned after water damage. Photographers at *The Daily News* came back with photos of houses teetering on the edge of a disappearing dune. Sometimes residences fell into the surging ocean. No kidding.

The ocean is rising, and the storms are doing more damage. Many homeowners knew this when they excitedly made plans with architects and builders. But they keep building. Many news stories have resulted. Yet storms that require city, state, and federal services are expensive. Roads must be rebuilt; damaged sewer systems must be reconstructed. Many taxpayers are tiring of spending government funds to protect houses of millionaires who put up "No Parking" signs on public streets.

In terms of feature stories, every community has interesting people. One feature that I launched was "the new newcomers." It ran around Thanksgiving time and was loosely tied to the custom of recognizing newcomers to America. Its parallel was the New Englanders hosted by Native Americans and all that.

I would focus on one immigrant a day leading up to Thanksgiving. Readers liked these success stories.

Here is one story: One middle-aged woman, "Ling," had come from Vietnam two decades earlier and had managed to open and own two salons for nails and skin. Numerous members of her family worked there. She had fled Vietnam several decades before in a leaky boat filled with unkempt fishermen. Asked what her greatest concern was, she replied, "I was six months pregnant and couldn't swim."

Ling had worked hard and raised three girls. She died of cancer about a year after the story ran. One of her daughters told me that a framed copy of my story was placed near her bedside in her final days. "I am so glad her story was told," one of her grieving daughters said.

Another woman I profiled was Grace Connolly, a prominent lawyer in Newburyport. She had been Graciela Garcia when the family fled Cuba in the '50s.

"My father was boarding a plane for Miami when he was paged at the airline desk," said Grace. "He did not go back inside the terminal. If he had, he would have been arrested and probably killed." Grace grew up in Florida and met Jim Connolly of Newburyport when she was in law school. They married, had three girls, and she made a very successful life in New England.

I did stories on a service-station owner from Lebanon, a female doctor from Pakistan, a teacher-poet from the Dominican Republic, and a restaurant owner from China.

In 2014, Newburyport had its 250th anniversary. I launched a thirty-part series on the history of the community. This town was the birthplace of the Coast Guard (1790), and the busiest shipbuilding town in New England. As the great historian Samuel Eliot Morison said, "The lower Merrimac, in Newburyport, was undoubtedly the greatest shipbuilding center of New England in its period [*circa* 1815]."

My series offered stories on the waterfront, schools, businesses, churches, clubs, and hospitals. I learned that the library and the local historical society had hundreds of excellent photos. Photography was invented in about 1839, and some of the earliest photos were taken on the North Shore. Local collections hold scores of photos of ships, fishing boats, and waterfront commerce.

I left *The Daily News* in 2017. As had happened before, the new editor didn't like my style. This has been a recurring theme in my career. But I can't complain. I worked for close to forty-seven years in the business.

Remember the TV talk show host Sally Jessy Raphael? I heard she was fired thirty-three times, which meant she was hired about thirty-three times. Perhaps I should consider myself the SJR of New England print.

I've had more adventures than most journalists. The opportunity to write books in recent years has excited me.

By 2025, I had written seven books. Few will read the newspaper stories I have written. The books that I have written are in libraries around New England. My books on history will be available for many years.

Books written in recent years include the following: *Plum Island: A Vulnerable Gem* (Fonthill Media, 2022); *Merrimack: The Resilient River, An Illustrated Profile of the Most Historic River in New England* (Fonthill Media, 2021); *New England Coast Guard Stories, Remarkable Mariners* (History Press, 2020); and *Nautical Newburyport: A History of Captains, Clipper Ships and the Coast Guard* (History Press, 2017).

I also speak to community groups or on Zoom about my books, helping to educate the community about the health and history of the Merrimack River.

On a separate subject, I was inducted to the Maine Tennis Hall of Fame in 2019. What a thrill! I had written a tennis column in the *Portland Press Herald* in the '70s and again in the '90s.

Organizers noted that I had written more than 1,000 articles on Maine players, coaches, teams, and programs. At the catered ceremony in Portland orchestrated by Maine tennis veterans Don Atkinson and Chan Bearce, I said, "This is a great honor for me, not just as a journalist but as a person. I covered many of these events as a journalist. I am pleased I am an awardee. And I don't have to go back to the newspaper to file a story on this."

Others honored include Phil Cole, the late coach of the University of Southern Maine team; Dick McNaughton, perhaps the best player in the state during the '70s; Roger Gagne, a great player who wins age-group tournaments on the New England level; and Lynn Welch, Maine's best woman player and an honored USTA umpire who has called matches at the U.S. Open and Wimbledon.

Fans who traveled to Portland included Vicki, Leslie, Drew, and Nico, two, our grandson.

A major delight in my septuagenarian years is the success of our children.

Leslie is a journalist in New York. In 2021, she married Andi, a pleasant carpenter-type from Albania. She met him in Greece while she was on a writer's retreat. It took many months for him to get a visa to America. But shortly after the Biden Administration took over, the paperwork began to flow. They were married at beautiful Maudslay State Park in Newburyport, with the Merrimack River in the background. They have a house in western Connecticut.

Drew is in Somerville, Massachusetts. He is an administrator for a nonprofit organization that brings tennis and tutoring to the inner city. He is married to Natalia, a native of Bogota, Colombia, and as I write this their son, Nico, is six.

Regarding travel, Leslie has journeyed to all fifty states and a dozen countries. Drew has journeyed to two dozen countries, and has lived in Ecuador, Colombia, Tanzania, and the Dominican Republic. In those foreign lands, he was doing humanitarian work for nonprofit organizations.

Vicki's life career has been one of remarkable success. She is much loved as the founder of Newburyport Adult and Community Education. She is also the founder and co-director of the Newburyport Literary Festival. She is among the most loved residents of Newburyport. She retired in 2023 at the age of seventy-seven.

Her mind and spirit are strong, though she has had eight orthopedic procedures in the past four years. I am happy to help her through each surgery and recovery. I'll say this again. Now that I am no longer traveling, I am home to support her—as she did me for many years.

Epilogue

In 2025, it is difficult for me to look back over five decades and believe that I had enough energy and daring to apply for jobs all over the country. And when I had a good job, sometimes I would leave it for a better position. My career in print was not the most successful. I didn't write for *The New York Times* or *The Washington Post*. But I have had an interesting run that included trips to several continents.

Because of media access, I have seen and written about a lot of Americana. If I were to deliver a graduation speech about "life," what would I say?

It is this: The best thing is family.

Many people have made this simple statement, but I repeat it here. Family is the best thing.

I had loving support: my grandmother, Edith Carter, of Rochester, N.Y.; my parents, Eloise and Clint Hendrickson of Demarest, N.J.; my sister, Dale, in Ann Arbor. My aunts and uncles in Long Island were great.

My children are now my best friends. My wife, Vicki, is a treasure. As I re-read this memoir, I am even more appreciative of her. What she went through to live with me. But here we are, fifty-five years later, still crazy after all these years.

Though newspapers are fading, there are thousands of jobs in professions relating to journalism. The number of communications positions is increasing at the corporate and university level.

Thousands of new positions are being created on social media. Sites like Google, Yahoo, Facebook, Instagram, and others are flourishing. Newspapers themselves do not dwell on the success stories of other media. Reporters are adept at pursuing negative story lines. But the number of journalism jobs is actually increasing.

Some of the best stories in recent years have appeared on online sites. Also, police misbehavior has been brought to light on scores of occasions by citizen-reporters. The #MeToo movement has brought down more sexual transgressors than a courtroom full of lawyers.

As always, the media is changing. Newspapers are fading, but social media has an explosive future.

And the media still offers a dynamic lifestyle. My goal was to have a fun and invigorating life. And that was my experience.